# To our readers

Peter Ralston

# Telling Stories

Apublication can shape an entire organization. Twenty years ago, the Island Institute's founders made what must have seemed a daring decision: produce a four-color annual magazine, handsomely designed and expensively printed that would explore, explain and celebrate the remarkable culture of Maine's islands. *Island Journal*, they reasoned, would be a meeting place for ideas, a forum for discussions, a venue for poetry and literature, a showcase for photography and the visual arts. The high quality of its content and design would attract attention (as new publications must to survive) and set the then-tiny Institute on a course for the future. Publishing that first *Journal* required more than half of the new organization's annual budget.

*Island Journal*, like the Island Institute itself, represented a new way of thinking about the isolated communities that stretch along the Maine coast. This new frame of mind was island-centered, for one thing: it took into account the wishes, traditions, feelings and beliefs of islanders. It questioned the wisdom of state policies that discriminated against island communities. It took seriously the natural resources on which islands depend; it considered the populated islands, at least, as human communities where people mattered at least as much as the rest of Creation.

*Island Journal* is a storytelling enterprise. From the start its contributors and editors have sought to illuminate island life through the eyes of those who live it. Their stories were (and are) the very essence of what this publication and the Island Institute itself have sought to celebrate and enhance.

Twenty years on, we believe more firmly than ever in the importance of islanders, their communities and their stories. If *Island Journal* has been successful, it is because it has enabled them to share their stories with the wider world.

*The Editors*

# ISLAND JOURNAL

*The Annual Publication of the Island Institute*
*Volume Twenty*

*Cover: Peter Ralston*

*page 9*

*page 42*

*page 46*

*page 63*

*page 74*

*page 84*

**ISLAND
INSTITUTE**
*Publishers of* Island Journal *and* Working Waterfront

*Sustaining the Islands and Communities of the Gulf of Maine*

**ISLAND JOURNAL**

PUBLISHER
Philip W. Conkling

EDITOR
David D. Platt

ART DIRECTOR
Peter Ralston

COPY EDITOR
Esme McTighe

GRAPHICS RESEARCH
Cathy A. Caveney

DESIGN
Mahan Graphics, Bath, Maine

PRINTING
J.S. McCarthy Printers, Augusta, Maine

●

*Of all those who lived and died on the Maine coast
since the last issue of* Island Journal,
*three individuals stand out
for their great contributions to the Maine islands.*

*Edward A. Myers, 1917–2002*

*Ann C. Pingree, 1931–2003*

*Emily L. Muir, 1904–2003*

**ED MYERS** was best known for his accomplishments in shellfish aquaculture, but he really should be remembered as a mathematician. Numbers were a sharp tool that he used with great precision. "There are 6,000 regular Maine lobster-fisherpeople with 500 traps each, total 3 million traps," he wrote in a *Working Waterfront* column late in 1998. "...90 million trap hauls for half a pound a trap, total 45 million pounds @ $3 a pound = $135,000,000, and using 1,636,363 bushels of bait (which will average $15/bu if the herring doesn't show)—$25,545,400 for bait, and on 90 haul days $14,256,000 for fuel. So that's the fishery."

You can't sum up a whole economic sector more succinctly than that. Ed stretched our brains with such exercises for years, forcing us to think in new, disciplined, wonderful and sometimes strange ways.

**ANN PINGREE** was a sailor and a longtime summer resident of North Haven. She and her husband, Charlie Pingree, Sr., were among the first Founding Members of the Island Institute. From her porch at Iron Point overlooking the Fox Island Thorofare, Ann observed the comings and going of yachts along the archipelago with a sharp eye and a wry sense of humor. Of all that could be said of her life, she held the island communities she knew close in her heart. And like the Thorofare off her porch, her quiet waters ran deep.

**EMILY MUIR** was an artist and designer of houses, a peace activist, an early environmentalist who understood the true worth of islands. "If peace is a dream, war is a nightmare, and I have no intention of keeping still," she wrote *The Time of My Life*, the autobiography she completed last year at the age of 98. Emily Muir distinguished herself as an artist in paint, stained glass, mosaic and other media; she saw to it that three beautiful islands would enjoy permanent protection; she helped found the Island Institute. At the Institute she established the Emily and William Muir Fund to provide opportunities for students, teachers and community leaders in island and remote coastal communities.

*The lives of Emily Muir, Ed Myers and Ann Pingree, and their willingness to share those lives with the rest of us, were gifts of incalculable value. In a very small way, we return those gifts by dedicating Volume 20 of* Island Journal *to them.*

Peter Ralston

# FROM THE HELM

## PHILIP W. CONKLING

As the 20th issue of *Island Journal* goes to press, I admit that 20 years is a long time to keep doing the same thing. But then anything really worthwhile, especially in Maine, takes time and patience to accomplish. And although much has changed since we started out, much abides, as Tennyson wrote more than a century ago.

Twenty years ago it was not uncommon to be asked in places like Augusta or Washington by people who should have known better, "You mean, people actually live on Maine islands in the winter?" And, incredulously, "What do they do when the summer's over?" Or, "Why should anyone help communities where people choose to be so isolated?" Twenty years of reminding mainlanders that Maine island culture is important on its own terms, and is alive and well besides, has paid off in at least one respect: we don't have to confront questions like that quite so often. This kind of progress is hard to quantify in a list of accomplishments. But I'd like to think *Island Journal*, *The Working Waterfront* and the Island Institute have contributed to a general recognition and appreciation across Maine (and elsewhere) of the admirable values and traditions of persistence, independence and interdependence that characterize the island way of life.

In fact, looking back over the span of two decades, I can say that island culture has never been livelier and healthier than it is today. I have been out and about in many island communities this winter and am impressed, even astounded, at how the collective energy islanders and their friends have invested in their communities recently is so evident.

Long Island, Casco Bay, became Maine's 495th independent town ten years ago this July. The argument against its secession was that a population of 125 year-round residents was too small to sustain itself without the kinds of government services and tax base provided by Portland. Today Long Islanders have paid off their long-term debt to Portland (years early) and have managed to maintain town services without raising taxes once. Along the way they have acquired and operated a well-equipped emergency rescue boat that has saved more than one life. They are about to complete a stunning new community center and library, connected to their two-room schoolhouse. The new building will serve as the vital nerve center and multiple-use space for everyone on Long Island.

Next door to Long, Chebeague Islanders have become Maine's leading advocates for innovative approaches to tax reform—as well they must. The recent revaluation in the town of Cumberland, of which Chebeague is a part, could irreversibly alter the character of the community as long-term residents, fishermen and boatbuilders are quite literally taxed, not just off the waterfront, but off the island. It's a life and death issue for them, and their energy, passion and imagination have captured the

*Continued on page 94*

## NATHAN MICHAUD

*Eastport's fake statue. Photo courtesy of
Ed French,* Quoddy Tides.

There's a statue in Eastport that isn't real. The statue is a 15-foot-tall bearded fisherman in a sou' wester and oil jacket, cradling a fish. It's hard to miss. But visitors to Eastport don't always know that the statue isn't real, that it's made of fiberglass and Styrofoam, that it doesn't have much history, that it doesn't actually commemorate anything. Maybe they get a whiff of its unreality— a sense that it's somehow out of place, that it's just a little too striking, a little too colorful, a little too cartoon-ish—but they let it go because, after all, why would a statue that isn't real be in downtown Eastport?

*Scene from* "In the Bedroom." *Photo courtesy of Miramax.*

*Thurston's Lobster Pound, miniaturized in Arizona (note palm trees).*

It's not a bad question. The short answer is that the statue is a prop left behind from the production of "Murder in Small Town X," a television series shot in Eastport in the spring of 2001. The long answer is a bit more complicated.

For the filming of the series, which combined elements of so-called "reality" TV with a more traditional murder-mystery plotline and aired on the Fox network later that summer, Eastport posed as the fictional town of "Sunrise, Maine." Its downtown was painted brightly, all lit up and re-populated by an oddly multi-cultural group of people (it was still supposed to be downeast Maine, after all). The real Eastport has seen tough times lately: many downtown store fronts are still vacant and the streets in non-tourist months are dead quiet at night. But during the two months of filming there, things were hopping around the clock. In fictional Sunrise, all the store fronts were occupied (albeit with strange and mildly spooky businesses like "Sundown Casket Company'" and "Sparky's Museum of Taxidermied Wonders"). There was even a hip nightclub, neon-lit and well-attended. While dressed up as Sunrise, Eastport always had something going on, with people busily setting up or taking down lights or camera tracks, and actors being shuttled everywhere. Yet when the last scenes had been filmed, and the whole mess of people and equipment was gone as suddenly as it had appeared, Eastport seemed quieter than ever. The last echoes of the noise were long gone by the next winter, and the melancholy of the empty store fronts was only enhanced somehow by the strange optimism of their new, bright paint. Today, even the colorful paint is gone, but the unreal statue of the fisherman remains.

## HOLLYWOOD'S MAINE: THE WAY LIFE SHOULD BE

People talk about the "magic" of Hollywood movie-making. That's all well and good, but there's also something about it that's just plain weird and contrary to the way most people do things. The weirdness multiplies when it's contrasted with life in coastal Maine. Generally speaking, things became the way they are around here for reasons that had very little to do with how things look. In the world of work from which so many of our coastal villages grew, form rarely stood much of a chance if it ever dared to cross function.

In movie-making the whole idea is to go the other way around. Exterior images are mimicked in order to imply the less tangible things behind them. Beat-up hands have to signify—in an instant—a life of hard work. And while it's nice if your actor happens to have beat-up hands from a life of hard work, it's far from necessary (not to mention pretty unlikely)—a little make-up, or better still, a quick cut-away to a real pair of beat up hands, and the actor assumes a history that isn't his. Of course filmmakers are obsessed with image and illusion—that's their currency. It just somehow seems so un-Maine.

Watching a production when it moves into town can give you pause. Seeing a team of people spending hours and hours "aging" a newly-constructed building façade by beating on it with hammers and

*Shooting "Murder in Small Town X" in Eastport. Photo courtesy Ed French,* Quoddy Tides.

*Shooting "Storm of the Century" in the miniature lobster pound.*

paint scrapers, for example, you might find yourself reflecting on the time and effort you put into painting your own house in order to achieve precisely the opposite effect.

It's weird when the reality of Maine isn't "real Maine" enough for a movie. When, as Thom Willey, a professional assistant cameraman and native of Southwest Harbor, says "they come into a small fishing village like Southwest Harbor, and completely changed it in order to make it look like a small fishing village like Southwest Harbor." Willey is alluding to the production of "Storm of the Century," a made-for-TV movie series written by Stephen King and shot in and around Southwest Harbor in the winter of 1998. Willey has worked as an assistant cameraman in productions all over the country; in Maine he's worked on the sets of "Storm of the Century," "Murder in Small Town X," "Cider House Rules," "Graveyard Shift" and "Langoliers." Consequently, he's more than familiar with this phenomenon of authenticity enhancement. But maybe it's a little stranger when your own hometown is tweaked and added-to to increase its legitimacy on the screen. Bring out the fish nets and buoys, and hang 'em all around. Lobster traps are good, too, especially if they're the wooden ones nobody uses anymore.

Stranger still, the film company painstakingly re-created their re-creation of downtown Southwest Harbor inside a sugar beet warehouse in Toronto, and shot many scenes there. About 50 people from town took a bus up to see it, and reported that the replication was exact to the last detail. "It was eerie," said one local business owner. "Until I looked up and saw a roof, it was like I was in Southwest Harbor."

Michael Radcliffe, owner of the F.W. Thurston Company Lobster Pound in Bernard, turned over his wharf, from which he buys lobsters and sells bait and fuel, to crews from both "Storm of the Century" and "Cider House Rules."

"They did a lot of work to make things quaint," he says. While Radcliffe spent some time hanging around the set and offering the crew advice ("both solicited and unsolicited"), he soon resigned himself to the notion that the way things actually looked and worked at a Maine lobster pound didn't really interest the movie makers.

"We work kind of haphazardly around here sometimes and maybe things don't end up looking too sharp," he says. "If you're looking at it from a director's point of view maybe it needs to be touched up a little to make it look like it's supposed to look to a guy from the Midwest. People have pre-conceived notions about what small Maine coast fishing villages look like, and it's the director's job to make it look that way. That's how the producer explained it to me: 'We don't want to make it look 100 percent authentic, we want to

*Image and illusion are the currency of filmmaking. Photo courtesy of Ed French,* Quoddy Tides.

*"Storm of the Century" crew at the full-sized Thurston's Lobster pound, Bernard (note wind machine at left). Photo courtesy of Michael Radcliffe.*

make it look like people think it's going to look.'"

Ed French, the editor of Eastport's twice-monthly newspaper, *The Quoddy Tides*, is philosophical about the way his town was represented in "Murder in Small Town X," noting that there was little reason to expect a film company from away to value the same aspects of Eastport the locals did. "Much of the local flavor was gone by the end of the process," he said. "But I suppose that's always a risk when you have a group come in with their own ideas about what they want to do to a place that you're not going to have it portrayed as it really is. I suppose there's a little disappointment [among locals] that [the filmmakers] don't see the value of what's here. But people have their own ideas about what places are."

And it's not as if these alterations are made in a conceptual vacuum. As Lea Girardin, director of the Maine Film Office, says, "location is character." Location, in other words, is just another tool for telling a story, advancing a plot, moving things toward a resolution. Film is a medium, which in many ways resists depth; while a novelist can spend pages describing a setting before any action happens, a filmmaker has maybe three quick

*To have a murder, you need a corpse.*
*Photo courtesy of Ed French, Quoddy Tides.*

shots, then has to rely on the audience to connect the dots between those separate images. Look around the room you're in now: which three images would you choose to stand in for the whole place? It often depends on who your audience is, and their understanding of iconography. It's no wonder so many filmmakers lean on cliché—it is in many ways a universal language.

"There are stereotypes everywhere. It is always a matter of degree," says Todd Field, director of "In the Bedroom," a critically acclaimed, low-budget film shot in and around Rockland and Camden in the

spring of 2000. Although Field, an Oregon native who has lived in Owls Head year-round since 1998, quite successfully avoided common stereotypes about Maine life in his film, he understands that in general, stereotypes exist for good reason. "There are fishermen I know who are very consciously walking and talking anachronisms. They enjoy living within the framework of a culture. This is true in all parts of the world. Yes, Romans enjoy the fact that they are expected to pinch the backsides of attractive young women—spend some time in Italy; it's a fact. These are cultural markers. You can call them stereotypes if you want, or cliché. I remember asking a Parisian the actually definition of the word 'cliché.' He said it 'affirms the consistency of culture… only you Americans who have no culture use it in a derogatory manner.'"

## ACT NATURAL

Field's point that stereotypes are not always something forced on a place or people from the outside is a good one. Stereotypes can be something closer to a negotiation between two vantage points; in classic (and some would say clichéd) Maine jargon, a kind of agreement between ideas "from here" and "from away." Like people in other places long accustomed to the dramatic contrasts that accompany seasonal tourism, some Mainers have long been adept at performing as themselves when the occasion arises. More often than not, it boils down to good economics—if tourists are seeking local flavor and they think you have it, well, why shouldn't you use that to your advantage?

"Often you're dealing in smoke and mirrors," says Maine author and literary scholar Sanford Phippen. "For example, my grandfather was a great folk hero who put on his act for folks down at Hancock Point. I remember him coming home and going on about something and my grandmother saying to him 'you're not down on Hancock Point now—don't give us that crap!'"

Phippen calls the differences in perspectives between what he says are now four distinct Maine populations—natives, old summer people, new summer people and tourists—"instant drama." Like the proverbial blind men and the elephant, each group has a hold on a different part of Maine, and is reporting often radically different findings. These conflicts, Phippen notes, form the dramatic foundation of many stories set here; he traces some of the inspiration for his own writing to the attention he paid to these differences while growing up in Hancock.

"As a little boy I was always fascinated by the coming and going of the summer people," Phippen says. "I wanted to know where they came from and why they came here… The social dynamics are very different, and when the summer people would arrive here they would insist—as they still often do—that their dynamic superseded the natives'."

By shifting back and forth between "here" and "away" perspectives in her 1946 novel *Spoonhandle*, Ruth Moore masterfully depicts a Maine island community's growing self-consciousness as the locals realize that their home is valued by others for reasons different from their own. For example, one of the book's more entrepreneurial island characters, Pete Stilwell,

*In "Murder in Small Town X," a car paid the ultimate price. Courtesy of Ed French,* Quoddy Tides.

puts on his "simple Maine folk" act for wealthy city people interested in buying island land because he knows this flavor is part of what makes the area attractive to city people. But he also uses the act to disguise his own keen business mind so that he can better take advantage of the situation. In a particularly memorable scene, Pete writes to a Baltimore man interested in buying land and riddles the letter with intentional misspellings and backwoods grammar:

*Pete read the letter carefully, took out his pen and crossed an 's' off the word 'guess,' then folded the sheet and put it into an envelope.*

*There, he said with a chuckle. That ought t'fetch him.*

The irony being, of course, that the "authenticity" the Baltimore man finds so attractive is in fact at least partly a performance of his own expectations. Such has

been the game in Maine and places like it for years—identity or character is more a conversation than a quality.

When Hollywood adapted *Spoonhandle* into the movie "Deep Waters" (filmed in part on Vinalhaven in 1947), the story's multiple layers and complexities of performance and perspective were all dropped. A novel praised for realism of the highest order was reduced to a fairly trite story about a boy and his love of the sea, set against a backdrop of a stereotypical small Maine fishing community. Little wonder that Moore, who had been hired as an advisor to the production, broke her contract and vowed to have nothing to do with the movie. Some say this got her blacklisted in Hollywood. Either way, she never worked in movies again. It was probably for the best.

*Dana Andrews and Cesar Romero (right) in Carvers Harbor, Vinalhaven, 1947.*

'Vacationland.' There are narrative films and there are documentaries. 'In the Bedroom' is the former."

Sometimes, of course, stereotypes are just lazy shorthand. On the one hand, it all seems pretty harmless—we Mainers find a lot of joy in making fun of caricatures, in fact. But on the other hand, perceptions of Maine are no trivial matter. Since tourism is now the state's biggest industry, perceptions translate into big money. And not unrelated to the way Maine is marketed to tourists are the many important battles being fought throughout the state in local planning boards and the Legislature alike—battles over aquaculture, cell-phone tower siting or land use—that boil down to the question of who gets to decide what Maine is supposed to look like.

## "A BIG, FAST MACHINE"

Once a year, Lea Girardin packs up her pictures of beautiful Maine settings and flies to L.A., where she displays them at the Location Expo. There, she and representatives from the film offices of all 50 states and many countries vie for the attention of thousands of filmmakers looking for the right place to shoot their movie. The Maine Film Office has two full-time employees and a small operating budget. As a division of the Office of Tourism, which itself is a division of the Department of Economic and Community Development, the Film Office has a clear and completely legitimate mission: bring Hollywood money to Maine. Film, after all, is pretty clean industry: ideally, movie companies coming into town will take nothing but pictures and leave nothing but footprints—and money.

A production can pump a lot of money into a place in a short time. In addition to paying for the use of specific

To their credit, many filmmakers do go the extra mile to achieve realism. For "In the Bedroom," which included several lobstering scenes, Field retained the services of his Owl's Head neighbor, lobsterman Charles Stone III, to teach actors Nick Stahl and Tom Wilkinson how it's done.

"We took them out to haul and had them pick traps," Stone says. "We had them out there for three, four hours at a time. I didn't show them much mercy—hey, they wanted to learn. We taught them how to steer a boat, we even had them gaff buoys and haul up traps, and we had to get them all geared up so they looked professional."

In addition to having Stone work with the actors, Field followed Stone around taking notes on his "wharf talk," and grilled him about details of the lobstering industry (the film's title actually came from a conversation Field and Stone had about lobster behavior in the different chambers of a lobster trap). Despite all the work, Stone says any lobsterman who sees the film will know that the actors are greenhorns by the way they pick traps, for example ("If you watch, you can tell, the way he picks up the crabs by the back legs and all"), or stack lobster crates. "But for people who had never done it," he says, "they did pretty good."

And for an audience that's never seen it done, what's the difference? Ultimately, every choice in a film production has to withstand the scrutiny of an intense cost-benefit analysis. Is convincing the small percentage of lobstermen in the audience sufficiently important to justify the money and effort it would require to convince them? Even the most earnest attempts at authenticity often have to settle for "authentic enough."

Some times these choices are based on practical considerations, but other times, they're artistic license. The Camden and Rockland that appear in "In the Bedroom," for example, are conspicuously absent of summer traffic, even though the film is set in late summer.

"I recall toying with the idea of 'summer people,' " Field explains. "Ultimately this idea died. I suppose it has to do with the fact that I am more interested in my neighbors who work three jobs without complaint, so that they can continue to reside in this part of the world, than the people who drive up and down Highway One looking for quaint. When the tourists arrive in town each year, I am absent. We spend the summer out of the fray—on an island. For precisely this reason, I do not think of Rockland, Thomaston and the like as summer haunts, even though I know damn well that they are the heart of

*Downstreet, Vinalhaven, 1947. Photos and poster courtesy of Vinalhaven Historical Society (5).*

*For "Deep Waters," a novel praised for its realism was reduced to a fairly trite story about a boy and his love of the sea.*

locations, compensating people for their trouble and spending money on food and lodging for the cast and crew, a production can contract locally for set construction, transportation, extras and technical advisors.

It seems unlikely that many towns would welcome productions if it weren't for the promise of money. Having Hollywood around can be fun for a while, but the pure force with which it can consume a place, closing streets and shutting down businesses, can be overwhelming.

"It's a very big, fast machine," says Andy Arey. "If a film company is doing anything at all, there isn't a person in the community they're not sooner or later going to come into contact with." In addition to running an island forestry company in Thomaston, Arey has worked a great deal as a location scout for commercials, magazine shoots and such feature films as "Signs of Life," "Bed and Breakfast" and "Man Without a Face."

Arey knows from experience that all film companies aren't created equal: "For 'Man Without a Face,' for example, they couldn't have been better—they backed it up 100 percent. We completely took over Rockport. It was a period film, so everything had to look like 1967. We dressed every store front on Main Street, and we built a whole set on the waterfront. Some businesses were used as locations (and compensated) and some weren't. So we bought the door for every business we didn't take over. I sat down with the owner and said, 'Look, we're going to take over Main Street for the next week, and obviously we don't want to compromise your business, so how much do we have to pay you a day to make you happy?' But a lot of film companies wouldn't have done that— they would have got the blessing of the town to do what they want and then take advantage of it."

Lea Girardin's advice is the same for communities considering welcoming a production and for citizens thinking about allowing the use of their home or business: know what you're getting into. "Every production has a different culture and a different bottom line," she says. "Most of the productions we've had are great and worked pretty well with the communities. We've had maybe three in the last 12 years that have been really hard, where I felt like the production team didn't really come in with a very good attitude toward the town or the people....What makes a project successful, even a big and difficult one, is pre-planning. The production company and the town or the landowner need to be absolutely clear about what they want and don't want. A town is well within their rights to say 'No, we don't want that.' There are contracts that have to be signed. Even though it has this glitz around the edges, it's still a business deal."

When a big Hollywood production comes to a small Maine town, stereotypes on both sides can create expectations that aren't always met. "I don't know if there's a 'downeast Maine type,' or an 'L.A. type,' " says Willey, who has a foot planted in each world, "but I think we each have our own stereotype of the other." Sometimes the surprises are pleasant. When the "Deep Waters" crew and cast—which included Cesar Romero and a young Dean Stockwell—came to Vinalhaven in 1947, much was made in the local paper about their being "real folks," who stayed in locals' homes, went to barn dances and even helped with chores.

As a location scout—essentially the mediator between film companies and communities—Arey deals a lot with expectations. When the producers of "Signs of Life"—a story about a wooden boatbuilder being driven out of business by the industry's shift to fiberglass—saw the "classic older-style lobsterboat" they wanted to shoot tied to the wharf in Stonington Harbor, Arey found the boat's owner, a lobsterman just in from one of the islands for groceries, and asked his permission: " 'Yeah, yeah,' [the lobsterman] says. 'That sounds like fun—I'd be glad to do it.' So we go off from the conversation," Arey says, "and four or five minutes later he's pulling on my shirt. I turn around and he says 'Ah, I don't mind you using my boat, but you're not going to blow it up, are you? Because if you blow up my boat, I'm going to have to have another.' "

*Continued on page 71*

*The movie adaptation of Ruth Moore's novel "Spoonhandle" was filmed in part on Vinalhaven in 1947.*

# Island Son

## For three decades, Sonny Sprague has stayed the course

BOB MOORE

Like every community on the Maine coast, Swan's Island has seen its share of change in the past 30 years. In most places, change came on like a supertanker, with a force and momentum that made steering difficult.

Swan's Island has been fortunate to have island son Myron "Sonny" Sprague in the wheelhouse. His soft-spoken manner and quiet persistence have guided this island community over shoals and through rough waters for over three decades. His long-range vision and hard work are proof that island communities can thrive when they act for the collective good. The key to it, Sonny says, is to be in it for the marathon, not the sprint.

*Island Aquaculture succeeded where others had failed. "We could do this better," Sprague said. He was right. Photographs by Peter Ralston (2).*

14

*Being a grandparent is a favorite occupation these days.*

ed a limit, but one that was enforceable and effective. That took a lot of discussion, and the process was time consuming and frustrating. "They—Sonny—stuck with it," says Apollonio. "They talked to fishermen from other ports like Bass Harbor and Stonington. That was not an easy thing to do. But it was clear they meant business."

If negotiating with neighboring communities on Mt. Desert and Deer Isle was difficult, the problem was compounded by the dicey need to convince a few dissenting Swan's Island neighbors that it was good for them too. Sprague needed to come to DMR with a semblance of unanimity in order to sell the commissioner on the idea. "[The commissioner] was for it, but not the way we were," says Sprague. "But we worked and we worked, and he could see we were sincere. It took years."

Where a sprinter might have gotten winded early on, the trap limit came through in the long run. Reflecting on that process, Apollonio sees Sonny Sprague as "a good example of a person who can talk in such a way as not to antagonize people. He can keep a discussion going and doesn't shut it off. His motivation is the survival of the Swan's Island community as something other than a summer community—as year-round and economically viable. Fortunately there are people like Sonny Sprague around that act out of no motivation other than for the good of the community. That's where the progress comes from. We are fortunate."

What motivates Sonny Sprague is nothing less than preserving Swan's Island's long-term viability as a year-round community. Not many mainland towns ever need to ponder that kind of question, because it isn't as crucial. Jobs can be had in the next industry or the next town over. An island's life and its vitality as a functioning community—with schools, churches and stores—is inextricably tied to how islanders make a living. And the options are fewer when you live offshore.

Sprague sees all of Maine's 14 year-round island communities as different. "There's not a one of them that's alike. The only thing they really have in common," says Sprague, "is you walk too far, you're going overboard." Beyond the geography lesson, Sprague recognizes the paramount importance of a stable year-round population. That means jobs. "You've got to have kids to keep the school going," says Sprague. "If the island economy fails, the year-round community and its businesses are at risk and could change drastically."

## AHEAD OF THE CURVE

Two examples of Sprague's vision and tireless campaigning for Swan's Island stand out. The first came in 1984 when the state permitted Swan's Island to enact an exclusive lobstering zone around the eastern

and southern shores of Swan's Island off to the three-mile limit. Anyone who wanted to fish in the zone, whether local or mainlander, also had to comply with a trap limit. In his characteristic humility Sprague doesn't take credit for this decisive move. "There were others that had the vision, they just probably needed someone foolish enough to jump out, and that was me," he laughs.

"Trap limits were inevitable and Sonny Sprague could see the time coming," says Spencer Apollonio, who was Commissioner of the Maine Department of Marine Resources (DMR) during that time. "He saw fishing pressure coming from all around. Island communities like Monhegan, Isle au Haut, Frenchboro and Swan's Island are going to get squeezed. Unless something gets done they will lose. Sonny Sprague was the leader in getting it done for Swan's Island."

Most of Swan's Island's fishermen agreed they want-

*"You learn from mistakes, both your own and those of others," says Sprague, who was a Swan's Island selectman for 25 years.*

*Tending algae tanks at Island Aquaculture.*

## SALMON AQUACULTURE

Sonny Sprague deals with change by anticipating and working with it. The second example of this was bringing salmon aquaculture to Swan's Island. As selectman in the late 1980s, Sprague was searching hard for ways to diversify the island's lobster economy. Offshore islands are poor incubators for most industries, so when Mariculture Products, a salmon aquaculture company with a proposal to bring fish farming to the island, approached Swan's Island it seemed like a good fit.

Opposition to change was intense. At one point it looked as if the federal government would not issue the necessary permits for the fish-farming site until too late in the season to start. Sprague recounts walking into the office of the Army Corps of Engineers in Augusta, where Jay Clements, the Corps' project reviewer, greeted him with, "Sonny, will you call those people down on Swan's Island off of the damned phones? You have your temporary permit! In another month the permanent permit will be here." It was.

The failure of the Mariculture Products salmon operation after two years, and that of the bank's hired team a year later, gave birth to the third, and perhaps most striking, example of Sprague's vision and tireless leadership.

With allies gained while working with the Island Institute, Sprague got the backing and loan guarantees to buy 12 salmon pens and 38,000 fish, and Island Aquaculture Company (IAC) was born. In its time IAC brought 12 full-time jobs and 20 part-time, seasonal jobs to Swan's Island. The seasonal work was processing salmon at the Quarry Wharf plant in Minturn. "It wasn't the best job in the world, but it went to places where there wouldn't have been money," says Sprague. "I call it kerosene and Christmas money. Back then lobster fishing wasn't as good, and a lot of them were wives of fishermen that needed to work."

The success of Island Aquaculture defied the predictions of industry pundits and outsiders who had watched two teams of "experts" in the field fail. How could islanders succeed? The average size fish produced on Swan's Island was a slight 6.75 pounds. "The prevailing opinion of the aquaculture industry was that Mariculture Products and Key Bank lost money because of the winter chill factor—that the site was too cold to grow salmon," recalls Island Institute president Philip Conkling. "Sonny was convinced it wasn't the water temperature, it was mismanagement."

The first year after Sprague took over as general manager, he and his crew were able to grow eight-pound salmon. The venture ultimately became profitable, thanks in no small part to Sprague's keen attention to detail. "He watched it like a hawk, and said 'we could do this better than them,'" says Conkling. "And he was right."

Island Aquaculture Company was bought out by Atlantic Salmon of Maine in the year 2000. Atlantic Salmon of Maine sold out to Fjord International in 2002. These days Fjord employs Sprague in a public relations capacity, as salmon aquaculture's "ambassador" to the fishing industry. His role exploits his proven knowledge and skills at politicking and diplomacy, and he travels around to fishing towns citing his firm conviction that lobstermen and salmon farmers are more alike than different. Though not directly involved in Swan's Island politics, he continues to fret for the future of his island home: he serves on the Board of Directors of SAD 76 because he wants to make sure every island child gets a good education. "It's awfully hard to tell a young child that he should get a good education when he can go out and fish 20 traps in an hour and get 100 dollars," says Sprague. "What really scares me is now is the increased pressure on the lobster fishery as a result of modern technology, along with what I consider to have been a poorly thought-out trap limit statewide. If fishing goes on the blink, a lot of the families will have to leave and without a good education they will not be able to compete in today's job market. An education is nothing but an insurance policy on quality of life."

As a veteran island watcher, Conkling marvels at Sprague's ability not just to raise fish where others couldn't, but also to bring about change so deliberately to an island community time after time. "His organizing principle is to put community ahead of the individual. That's a hard sell anywhere, but it can be especially tough on an island. Ultimately, islanders know better than anyone else that no one is an island. They rise and fall together. Sonny has been able to mobilize that more effectively than any leader I know of. It's his genius to know where the rocks are, and wait for high tide or the right wind to get around them."

While serving in the Maine Senate, Jill Goldthwait of Bar Harbor kept a newspaper photo of Sprague at a selectman's meeting pinned to the wall for inspiration. "Whenever things looked hopeless and I'd ask myself 'Can I hang in there?'" says Goldthwait. "I'd look at that picture and say, 'Yes I can.' He's my hero."

Ask Sonny Sprague how he was able to succeed in ventures where others had failed or dared not try, he replies, "You learn from mistakes, both your own and those of others. If you're smart enough to realize there are people in the world who are smarter than you are and you allow them to work with you and use common sense, you'll probably survive." Sound advice for mainlanders and islanders alike who are in it for the long run.

Sonny Sprague was a Swan's Island's selectman for 25 years before retiring in the fall of 1993. At town meeting the next spring he was honored with the presentation of a gold pocket watch. It was inscribed, "To an island son who gave more than just his time."

*Bob Moore writes regularly for Island Institute publications.*

# The Center of

## FOR CONTEMPORARY ISLAND ARTIST

EDGAR ALLEN BEEM

Islands, by their very nature, are isolated and circumscribed. Physically removed, surrounded by water and small enough to be known intimately by residents and visitors alike, islands tend to produce a concentration of attention that is fundamental to all visual arts. Of course, what artists on islands choose to concentrate on differs widely from artist to artist.

The most popular artists associated with coastal and island Maine—Winslow Homer, Rockwell Kent, Fairfield Porter, the Wyeths —have tended to work in a realist tradition focused on the landscape and the human figure, but there is a wide range of Maine island art beyond this narrative tradition. In selecting ten contemporary Maine island artists as a representative sampling of the art that lies beyond pure realism, I have been guided by something Fairfield Porter, a lifelong summer resident of Great Spruce Head Island, wrote back in 1974.

*"Perry Creek and the Thorofare"* Eric Hopkins, 1995
*6' x 4'*

# the Universe

## ART IS ALL ABOUT EDGES

*"Gotts Island, Maine," Henry Finkelstein, 1996
46" x 56"*

"For me," wrote Porter, "painting does not illustrate or prove anything; neither 'realism' nor 'abstraction' nor any of the categories invented by journalists. It is a way of expressing the connections between the infinity of the diverse elements that constitute the world of matters of fact."

With that dictum firmly in mind— that painting is essentially a way of expressing universal connections—it is easy to see the sweeping, soaring island paintings of North Haven native Eric Hopkins as images of the universe in microcosm. Hopkins paints as though North Haven were the center of the universe, the firmament whirling around Penobscot Bay with such velocity that land and sea are shaped into a big blue ball.

"Nature is just one big abstraction," enthuses Hopkins, the Maine artist most closely associated with "islandness." And what Hopkins tends to concentrate his attention on, whether painting from a plane in the sky or a boat on the water, are the curvilinear edges of things and the forms defined by these edges.

"What is an island? You're living on the edge," he says. "It's all about edges."

Brita Holmquist, who was eight days old when she first came her family's summer cottage on Islesboro's Gilkey's Harbor, agrees.

"The simplification is attractive to me. It really clears my brain," says Holmquist of island life. "The island is a place you can inhabit between the sky and the water. It's the safety edge."

But Holmquist insists, "Eric is wrong. Islesboro is definitely the center of the universe." That said, Holmquist admits, "There is the same intensity about the bay, where everything under the sun happens. He paints from the sky. I paint from a boat very low down."

Where Hopkins concentrates on edges and forms, however, Holmquist sees islands more in terms of pattern. Her emphasis on painting the rhythmic patterns of waves and clouds imposes an order on the island experience that imparts a sense of charmed regularity, animating the known world with the invisible forces of nature.

*"Cumulus Over Spruce Island,"*
*Brita Holmquist, 2002*
*12" x 18"*

Suzanne Heller, a year-round resident of Vinalhaven, creates her own sense of island charm by painting island people, places and plants with an almost child-like simplification. Whether making folksy portraits of island residents in oil or vignette-like landscapes in watercolor, Heller edits reality down to the bare essentials.

"Vinalhaven has allowed me this freedom," Heller writes. "I am able to see Vinalhaven's people and its landscape clearly, without interferences (except it's harder in the summer). It is a beautiful and pristine workplace and home."

The predominant style of painting in Maine is painterly realism, a brushy form of representational painting characterized by a free use of color derived from European Expressionism, American and French Impressionism and Abstract Expressionism. One of the most astute painterly realists on Maine islands is Henry Finkelstein, a lifelong summer resident of Great Cranberry.

Though frequent trips across to neighboring Gott's Island to visit his wife's family has opened the vistas of Finkelstein's paintings in recent years, what most char-acterizes his approach to island imagery is a preference for close and closed-in settings.

"I think I always paint intimate spaces," says Finkelstein. "I like to find overgrown, brambly gardens. I look for expansiveness in small places."

In an island landscape heavily browsed by deer, Finkelstein finds he has to seek out small cottage gardens and farmyards to get the kind of thickets and containment he seeks. Bicycling back from a day of painting, he frequently comes across fellow Cranberry artists Emily Nelligan and Marvin Bileck, the only artists on the island who tend to stay out later than he does.

Emily Nelligan has been called "the Emily Dickinson of painters," both because she is famously shy and because her magical charcoal drawings of Cranberry are at once extremely subtle and incredibly powerful. Looking at the island shores through sea fogs and gathering darkness, Nelligan captures the mysterious moodiness of islands as no one else does.

"The moment I first arrived on the island over 50 years ago, I felt at home," says Emily Nelligan. And though she is at

a loss for the words to describe this sense of belonging, islanders up and down coastal Maine will identify with that sentiment and recognize it in the soft focus of Nelligan's charcoals.

"Most of the time Emily and I are drawing side-by-side, only a few yards apart," says her husband, Marvin Bileck. "Her medium is charcoal, so she can instantaneously capture the lights and darks, the illumination and the shadows. I'm working with a line that is the opposite of that mass, but it is well suited for detailing the edge."

A master printmaker, Bileck explores the edges and outlines of island rocks with a deftness that elevates his perception of nature to an aesthetic experience. His etched lines are at one with the mineral architecture of the island shores.

An entirely different artistic impulse is made manifest in the art of Robert Indiana, the internationally-known Pop Art star who has made his home on Vinalhaven since 1978. Originally drawn to the island because one of his artistic heroes, painter Marsden Hartley, had lived and worked there, Indiana already had a well-established signature style when he arrived on Vinalhaven. Appropriating techniques from commercial art (block lettering, logo-like imagery, sign painter graphics), Indiana is a signifier, codifying his ideas and perceptions in a visual vocabulary all his own.

"Living on Vinalhaven for 24 years hasn't changed anything very much," says Indiana of the impact island life has had on his work.

But while his style remains unchanged since the 1960s, what Indiana has chosen to celebrate and commemorate in his art since moving to Maine does reflect his island life. He documented his first ten years on the island in a silkscreen series entitled "Decade: Autoportraits, The Vinalhaven Suite" and honored his hero Hartley in a series of 18 "Hartley Elegies." A trafficker in signs and symbols, Indiana brings to his new diamond-shaped painting "The Islands" (commissioned for the State Office Building in Augusta) the same inspired design sense that has made his "LOVE" paintings, prints and sculptures international icons. "The Islands" uses a blue-green palette not all that different from Eric Hopkins' but to graphic rather than descriptive ends.

Maine still has a hard time fully appreciating abstract art, perhaps because the evidence of hard work is not as obvious as in art where fidelity is the measure. And while Monhegan Island is still best-known as the stomping ground of realists such as Robert Henri, George Bellows, Rockwell Kent and Jamie Wyeth, Monhegan has long been one of the few places where abstraction has thrived, most notably in the art of painters such as Joseph DeMartini, Murray Hantman, Michael Loew, William McCartin and, most recently, William Manning.

Bill Manning is an Abstract Expressionist painter who lives and works most of the year in Portland, but for 40 years most of his paintings have been inspired by the one to two months a year he spends on Monhegan. While it might not be obvious to the casual viewer, Manning's paintings, while non-representational, are nonetheless direct responses to the natural dynamics of light, sky, water, clouds, landforms and vegetation on that monumental little island. What you are seeing in a Manning panting may be the recollection and interpretation of the col-

*Untitled, Marvin Bileck. undated.*

*"The Islands," Robert Indiana, 2002*
*84" x 84"*

*"No. 1099," William Manning, 2001*
*23" x 23"*

*"Twist," David Row, 2002*
*32" x 40"*

*Untitled, acrylic on canvas,*
*Maurice Colton III, 2000*
*20" x 16"*

## John Wulp: "I knew at once that I was going to live there"

On his way to visit Great Spruce Head Island, inspired by viewing a Fairfield Porter show at the Whitney Museum in 1984, John Wulp accidentally wound up sailing into Pulpit Harbor on North Haven. "When I stepped foot on the island," he recounts in the monograph on his life and art, *John Wulp*, recently published by CommonPlace Publishing, "I knew at once that I was going to live there."

Live on a Maine island Wulp did, but not North Haven. Unable to find his dream "little white New England cape beside the water," he took the realtor's advice and explored nearby Vinalhaven where he quickly found a place to his liking. The house came with 60 acres and a "beautiful old ruined orchard." The apple trees would provide subject matter for a number of remarkable watercolors and acrylics.

Born in New Rochelle, New York, in 1929, Wulp has been painting since third grade. Busy as a theater producer and director in New York and elsewhere, he painted in fits and starts through the years, managing to turn out occasional portraits, landscapes and still lifes. Once settled on Vinalhaven he took up the brush with new vigor after a 10-year hiatus, painting exquisite studies of apple blossoms, lilacs, a bird's nest and rocks in Arey's Cove. He also continued with his portraiture, which

*"The Four Seasons: Autumn," John Wulp, 1994. Courtesy of the Frost Gully Gallery*

included a pair of likenesses of "two local ladies," Lucinda Ziesing and Lucinda Lang. The house itself, with its angled stairways and ceilings, provided material for luminous interiors.

Wulp's paintings of the apple orchard in all seasons stand among his greatest achievements as an artist. Employing a realist approach, he renders the complex branches with extraordinary skill.

Knowing the ups and downs of the artist's life, the artist may feel a certain kinship with these battered trees that manage to bear leaves each spring.

In addition to painting, Wulp produced, directed and wrote much of the community musical "Islands." He continues to work with island students on theatrical productions, but a recent exhibition at the William Beadleston Gallery in New York City and his current show at the Farnsworth Art Museum in Rockland (through July 13, 2003) have turned the spotlight on his artwork. Wulp's friend Eric Hopkins, who created the slide show for "Islands," is also the subject of a Farnsworth exhibition that runs until July 27.

–Carl Little

---

ors of twilight and dawn, fair skies and stormy, or the nautical palette of passing sails, painted hulls and lobster buoys.

"My work has changed dramatically over the years from the incredible organic structure of the island in line and black-and-white to color relationships," says Manning. "It took me 40 years to understand color better."

Maurice Colton III, who studied with Bill Manning 30 years ago, is a South Portland native who settled year-round on Matinicus in 1997 after spending the better part of two decades in New York City. A gestural painter greatly influenced by Jackson Pollock and Robert Motherwell, Colton brings the dynamics of action painting to bear on the physical reality of Matinicus. When he first visited the island 20 years ago, drawn there by a George Bellows painting of Matinicus rocks, Colton executed a series of watercolors of the shoreline rocks, but since moving permanently to the island he has returned to his abstract roots.

"I'm still very much rooted in the direction I started in art school—a strong, intuitive, vital connection to texture," says Colton. "Geometry never had any feeling

for me. It was a man-made construction. In reality, I see and sense life as a textural thing. It's like rocks. I love the idea of fragmentation. I'm on a rock. I'm on a mountaintop out here."

David Row, on the other hand, is very much inspired by the geometry underlying all natural phenomenon. Born in Portland and raised in Falmouth, Row now lives and works in New York City, but he has been summering on Cushing Island in Casco Bay all his life. Many of his very urbane abstract paintings are made in a studio overlooking Whitehead Passage.

"Working on the island is being surrounded by nature," says Row. "Nature is very important to me and to my work. It's all there, which is very different from in the city."

While the island influence is extremely subtle in paintings inspired by subatomic forms such as the double helix of DNA, it is there nonetheless. Two summers ago, for instance, Row mixed a palette of 200 colors by matching the hues of Cushing Island flora, fauna and rock formations. He also tends to work much later into the night on the island, such that many of his island paintings have

a nocturnal feel. Then, too, there is the most essential human condition of Maine islands—the isolation.

"I don't have a phone in the studio and I don't have the interruptions I have here in the city," Row explains, "so I have a deeper concentration when I'm there."

Living on the edge, becoming aware of rhythms and patterns, absorbing color relations, exploring line, form and texture, experiencing the intimacy, isolation and concentration of island life—all these manifestations of "islandness" tend to open artists, and indeed all of us, to a world beyond appearances. For in their compression of experience and perception, islands create a psychic reality parallel to their physical reality.

Painter Bill Manning could be speaking for any seasoned islander on any Maine island when he says of Monhegan, "The island still has the same aura to me. It has a very mystical feel to it. I still get the feeling that some supreme being has made this structure."

---

*Edgar Allen Beem is a freelance writer and art critic who lives in Yarmouth. He is the author of* Maine Art Now.

# Island of the
# BEAR CLAN

## Native Americans regain a sacred space

*Story and Photographs by*
DEBORAH DUBRULE

Library of Congress (2)

The end of their earth walk began with symptoms of smallpox and their immediate exile to the island white men named "Gordon's" in Big Lake.

Settling into canoes at the shore of the Passamaquoddy Tribe's main village, women, men, infants and children—wrenched from their families and friends, aching with fever, fatigue and pulsating blisters—paddled three-and-a-half miles across the lake's wind-lashed waters to reach the island. Everyone knew they would never return. Everyone knew they were paddling to their graves.

Victims of the last smallpox epidemic that almost destroyed the tribe in the mid-1800s, their uncounted bodies lie today in unmarked graves on what the Passamaquoddy call *Muwinwi Monihq,* Island of the Bear Clan.

*The Passamaquoddy Tribe allowed photographs to be taken of their sacred rites for the first time.*

*"It's like the Berlin Wall coming down… we never thought that this would actually happen,"* enthused tribal elder Jim Mitchell. *"But they say miracles do happen, and this is one of them."*

The Passamaquoddy Tribe considers this 26-acre island in the St. Croix River watershed to be sacred, and has coveted it for decades. But, like other Native American ancestral land in northeastern Maine, it has been owned by a string of corporations that controlled the nearby paper mill. Georgia-Pacific Corp. (G-P), one of those owners, refused repeated tribal offers to purchase the site.

Domtar Industries, Inc., which bought the mill two years ago, also refused to sell: instead, the Montreal-based company offered the island as a gift.

The gesture was unprecedented in Maine, and kindled hopes for a new era of friendship between neighbors. It also signaled new beginnings for the living and the dead: that of spiritual healing for the descendants of those who survived the epidemic; final peace for the souls of those who suffered and died there, whose last wishes were denied.

The healing was eerily displayed in the spring of 2002, when Domtar officials returned the island to the tribe at a formal ceremony on the Indian Township reservation near Princeton. During an event reminiscent of meetings that occurred between the tribe and their French allies three centuries ago, one Passamaquoddy chief greeted executives in French, company officials addressed leaders and guests in Passamaquoddy, the mill manager called the Indian nation the island's "rightful owners" and the tribe allowed photographs to be taken of their sacred rites for the first time.

Equally stunning, as the celebration began amidst ancient rituals intertwined with Christian prayer, and as tribal leaders shared a sacred pipe with executives, an eagle appeared from clouds in the west—the direction of Bear Island. The eagle is the most revered and sacred animal among American Indian nations.

A good omen, observed then-Rep. Donald Soctomah, the Passamaquoddy's delegate to the Maine Legislature, to 200 tribal members and guests. "We believe that our ancestors see through the eyes of eagles."

"It's like the Berlin Wall coming down…we never thought that this would actually happen," enthused tribal elder Jim Mitchell. "But they say miracles do happen, and this is one of them." Mitchell had long reminded members not to forget the sacrifices of smallpox victims, and entreated leaders to retrieve the island.

Mitchell, 84, is believed to be a descendant of the Bear Clan whose hunting territory included the island, and which was the first group hit when the last wave of smallpox decimated the tribe.

As those families—37 people—succumbed to the disease, infected members from the mainland joined them.

Written records about this, as well as earlier outbreaks that repeatedly ravaged Passamaquoddy people, do not exist, and tribal accounts stemming from oral traditions sometimes conflict. Mitchell's older sister, Delia Mitchell, is considered a central story-keeper of the event, which was rarely discussed until recently.

She recalls the tragedy as clearly as her fingers recall the memory of basket making. At 86, Delia Mitchell is almost blind but continues to weave brown ash baskets like those her ancestors delivered to white families who lived near her village. It was those families who ignited the epidemic, she said.

Natives who lived or camped on the islands made baskets, shoes, medicines and paddles, among other goods, to sell or swap for vegetables, beef or other foods with non-Indian farmers who had settled around Big Lake, Mitchell explains. According to her parents and grandparents, members of the clan contracted the disease while selling baskets to white people living across the lake. "There was a quarantine sign on the house, but the Indians couldn't read. So they went in and got [the disease]. People weren't educated then. They couldn't read or write."

Albert Dana, former tribal representative to Maine's legislature, remembers his father telling him the disease was unleashed intentionally by infected youths from Princeton. "It was a warfare system in those-

days," he said, describing white men who came to the village regularly to start fistfights with Indian residents. Like others, he recalls tales that the island was haunted. A hunting guide in the watershed for more than 50 years, 84-year-old Dana reflects, "That was a desolate place for someone who died from smallpox... But nobody knows exactly what happened there."

While some Passamaquoddies in the mid-19th century built homes on the mainland, others maintained their nomadic traditions, living and moving alongside the natural fish and animal migrations, often along the shores of islands. Delia Mitchell explained that people who lived in or around the village paddled to the islands "all the time to pick berries and fish and hunt and trap."

At least one boy from the Bear Clan was ashore when word of the legendary sickness reached the village and ended travel to the island. Mitchell says her grandmother took him in during the outbreak and, ultimately, raised him: his family perished in the disease's first sweep.

As smallpox whipped through the village, many victims hoped to stop its rampage by isolating themselves on the island, explained former tribal governor John Stevens. Some, however, were forcibly exiled. "If they tried to come back [to the village], they'd shoot at them."

Other victims were turned back too, reflects Mitchell: near death and unable to receive last rites, they desperately sought burial among their families who, converted to Catholicism by missionaries for two centuries, were laid to rest in the consecrated cemetery at Indian Township.

*The island's restoration to the Passamaquoddy Tribe "completes a circle," explains a tribal elder, referring to a Native tenet concerning the interconnectedness of all things and all beings.*

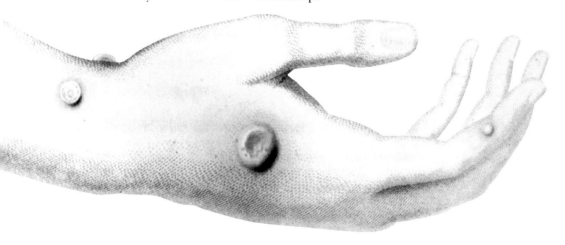

*At least one boy from the Bear Clan was ashore when word of the sickness reached the village and ended travel to the island. A woman took him in during the outbreak and, ultimately, raised him: his family perished in the disease's first sweep.*

The few survivors who attempted to return met gunfire as well, Stevens said. Their faces and bodies deformed by scars, they reportedly found refuge with Wabanaki Confederacy tribes in New Hampshire and Quebec.

Oral accounts do not include incidents of euthanasia or suicide but, nationwide, neither was uncommon among Native Americans. One written account in the West describes a group of survivors who killed themselves after viewing their faces in mirrors they bought from fur traders.

The word "smallpox" sent Indians and non-Indians running away, literally, for their lives. Though non-Indians had developed some resistance and could survive the highly contagious Variola major, Native Americans had no immunity; survival was rare.

Spread by air and physical contact, the virus has a 12-day incubation period during which victims suffer from headache, fever, nausea, back pain and skin rashes. Then, blisters form on face, hands and feet, and fill with pus. Declared one Mandan chief before he died, "[E]ven the [hungry] wolves will shrink with horror at seeing me."

Convulsions, delirium, pounding backache and 106-degree fever usually deliver an agonizing death. Deep skin craters and scars permanently mark survivors.

Reflects Stevens somberly, "People have conflicted emotions about the island and what happened at that time. It was a strange disease and they didn't know how to deal with it...maybe people will find some peace with this now."

Despite this anguished memory within their 12,000-year history, the tribe's actions likely prevented the extinction of the country's easternmost Indian nation.

Historians credit smallpox, delivered by European contact, as the greatest killer of indigenous people throughout North America, estimating that nine out of ten died from what today's military calls a bioterror weapon. In fact, Lord Jeffrey Amherst, commander of British forces during the 18th century French and Indian Wars, is often called "the father of germ warfare" because of his use of the disease to wipe out tribal communities. During the wars, he knowingly dispensed smallpox-infested blankets to Indians.

Today's smallpox vaccine was available in the early 1800s, but the Passamaquoddy—"wards of the state" until 1975—were not inoculated.

Infants and children were the most vulnerable to smallpox. Historically, they account for the greatest number of deaths worldwide.

By 1900, 16 of the region's 20 Wabanaki tribes were extinct from wars, smallpox and lesser ailments.

By 1910, only 110 Passamaquoddies had survived this holocaust, said Soctomah, adding that one report noted, "out of 250 births, 104 infants survived."

Anthropologists persistently predicted the tribe's extinction, he points out, noting that despite high birthrates, the Passamaquoddy population remained under 150 until the mid-1900s.

The number of dead on Bear Island is unknown, said Soctomah, who was instrumental in negotiating the island's return. "It's a number the elders didn't want to keep."

"[Native people] used to find skeletons and bones around the [island's] shore," said Delia Mitchell. "I guess some [tribal members] covered them up and buried the bones. When I was a little girl, we used to go there all the time to pray and have picnics."

She described seeing wooden crosses, lashed together with leather strips, that speckled the island and recalled a trip when they were scattered on the ground. "Animals must have chewed through the leather," she said softly.

An eight-foot white cross, erected by a priest several years ago who served this long-devout Catholic community, stands at the island's shore to commemorate the dead. Several mounds of earth mark gravesites, but burials were an unlikely priority for the dying, who were probably caring for children and infants. Not far from the cross lie the unmarked graves of infants.

*A cross on the shore commemorates the dead.*

Family groups like Mitchell's have made similar pilgrimages to the island—to pray, to hunt, to picnic, to fast—throughout much of the 20th century.

"The island's been used for spiritual cleansing and healing for years," explained longtime political activist and former Tribal Council member Wayne Newell. "It's a sacred space because of our connection to the people buried there. We have a strong connection to the spirit world there. The island is like a bridge [between the two worlds]."

Until last spring, the safety of this hallowed site was never assured. Legally, the Passamaquoddy were trespassers. In fact, tribal leaders had to seek permission from paper company officials to perform sacred rituals they conduct annually on the island to commemorate the dead.

Additionally, summer homes dot many island shores in Big Lake, a popular sportfishing area. So, while harvesting the timber-rich island was never practical economically, Maine's voracious summer cottage industry posed a threat to Bear Island and its scattered human burial sites.

"For years," Soctomah said, "[Georgia-Pacific] used the island as a leverage point on any kind of negotiations because they knew how much we wanted it. We offered to buy it. We offered to do anything to get it back."

Following decades of conflict, G-P's last tribal interaction involved a successful lawsuit against the tribe and the Penobscot Nation over internal water quality documents that included jail sentences for tribal governors. The lawsuit's outcome, tribal members believe, eroded tribal sovereignty.

Executives from Domtar, the second largest manufacturer of uncoated paper in the world, not only refused to join the lawsuit when it bought the mill, but demonstrated their intention to foster goodwill by returning the island with no strings attached.

The island's restoration to the Passamaquoddy "completes a circle," Newell explained, referring to a Native tenet concerning the interconnectedness of all things and all

beings. He said the tribe's sacred places, "places where we could connect spiritually," have been stolen or otherwise alienated. And, "because of the incident of smallpox, the island became a focal point where this connectedness can be maintained," he said. "So, it's come full circle—it's complete.

"This island has journeyed with us through all the difficult things that have happened to us. Like most of our land, it was alienated from us. In a sense, the reunion started when all those people got sick and died there, and it became the place where they were buried. We're now whole again," he said, adding that the tribe is placing the island in trust with the federal government, ensuring its protection.

Last spring, as the island moved into tribal hands, Debby Feck, the mill's first female manager and a fourth-generation employee, ended the last speech with the core sentiment that drew tribal members to the celebration that day: "*Apaciyawolotuwok ktlonapemuwak*—your relatives have returned to you."

But as festivities ended with a final prayer and boats awaited passengers who attended the first sacred pipe ceremony on Muwinwi Monihq under the tribe's stewardship, another eagle glided across the sunlight from the east—the direction of a new day, the direction of new beginnings.

A good omen—for the living and for the souls who returned from Muwinwi Monihq.

**Deborah DuBrule** *is a Maine-based freelance writer.*

*The paper company that had controlled Gordon's Island for decades returned it to the Passamaquoddy Tribe in a formal ceremony at Indian Township in the spring of 2002.*

# Hard times for the HORSE MACKEREL

## Maine's fastest fish may not be able to outrun its enemies

As the dog days of August approach in the Gulf of Maine, with massive aggregations of herring and mackerel churning the dark waters with glowing phosphorescence, and stratified, relatively calm conditions resulting in surface temperatures in the mid 60s in the western gulf, the giant bluefin tuna slip into our coastal and offshore waters. These eight-to-ten foot rockets of the sea are the fastest, strongest, most valuable, and now among the most vulnerable, of Maine's summer visitors.

The giant bluefin, or *Thunnus thynnus* (roughly translated as the "tuna of all the tunas"), is a seasoned long distance traveler, and Maine is but one annual option for this restless fish. With fish from the northwest Atlantic showing up in Norwegian, Mediterranean and Bay of Biscay waters, it is known that bluefin migrations can be both vast and fast.

Yet to fisheries scientists, bluefin travels remain remarkably enigmatic. Their peregrinations make for difficult management, with virtually every Atlantic country vying for a piece of the stock as they pass by. An international body is required that is willing and able to create and enforce conservation regulations across literally the entire expanse of an ocean, encompassing many different fishing gear types and cultures, and capable of restraining the human pressure for what is, pound for pound, the most valuable food animal in the world.

**Facing page: Photo by Bill Curtsinger**

*From the 1950s to the 1970s the Bailey's Island Tuna Tournament was an annual favorite.*

*Thirty years ago there was little market for tuna meat, which fetched prices that ranged from a nickel to a quarter per pound.*

Such a regulatory body does exist, but the execution of its mission has been flawed, and the tuna have been the ones to suffer. While the migratory tuna population visiting the Gulf of Maine has declined considerably since the mid-1990s, and prices have shrunk a bit as well, there are still a few indefatigable Maine fishermen who set forth each year to scan the waters, watching for the telltale wake, and hoping to hook or harpoon a giant.

The bluefin, or, as it was called in the past, the horse mackerel, was once regarded primarily as a nuisance. Large tuna would follow schools of mackerel or herring into weirs or seines, and then tear their way out. There was little market for the meat, although some heads and bellies were rendered for oil, or processed into pet or other animal food. Until the Second World War, fish were selling for the same price as bait mackerel. In the 1950s, commercial and sport fishing efforts increased rapidly, with new export and domestic markets developing. Pelagic long-lining in offshore Atlantic waters was introduced by the Japanese in 1956, and purse-seining in the New York area began in 1962, proving to be especially effective at catching juveniles. This category still comprises about 20 percent of the total catch, a fact that rankles many sports fishermen and conservationists, although the seiners are required now to target only the largest fish.

In the autumn of 1972, Japanese buyers first came to the docks of New England, after learning that the giant tuna taken in the northwest Atlantic had the ideal fat content for sushi and sashimi. Techniques and markets had been developed for flash frozen, overnighted, air-delivered tuna. In that year, Asian buyers offered an eye-catching $1.45 per pound, a startling increase from prices that had been running from a nickel to a quarter. This bounty led to greatly increased rod-and-reel fishing pressure, especially in Massachusetts, Maine and Nova Scotia. On-the-dock prices for tuna skyrocketed in New England during the boom economic times in Japan in the 1980s and early 1990s, exceeding $40 a pound. An individual fish could bring a fisherman tens of thousands of dollars. Even though the Asian economic downturn made memories of the highest prices, the fish are still very highly regarded. The record price for a single bluefin was reached in 2001, with the first fish of the year (which commands significant prestige and thus an artificially inflated price), a svelte, hard frozen, headless 440-pounder, selling for a cool $173,600.

## HARPOONS AND TOURNAMENTS

Maine fishermen have specialized in the artisanal method of harpooning, in which surface swimming tuna were harpooned by vigorous fishermen hurling spears by hand from long catwalk-like tuna pulpits rigged from lobster boats, thus taking (by choice) only the largest fish, and having no bycatch. This method of fishing has evolved from simple wooden harpoons to aluminum shafted irons bearing electric darts, which ensure a quick kill, but otherwise remains just as it always has, a game of stealth and skill, relying in the end on a steady eye, a carefully driven boat and a strong throw.

Lexi Krause of Monhegan Island has been hunting tuna in this way for nearly 30 years. Fishing from a point miles offshore has its advantages, as he starts closer to the grounds, and is able to judge and exploit breaks in the weather or fog. Noting that the tuna used to come closer to the island, Lexi remembers "standing on the cliffs on the back side of the island, and watching fish swim past right on the surface, and even seeing them occasionally right at the mouth of the harbor, even jumping right in the harbor on some occasions, such as Sherm Stanley's wedding day."

"We took that as a good sign," Krause recalls. He had one nine-fish day in 1988.

Muriel Hendrix

*Giant tuna in the northwest Atlantic have the ideal fat content for sushi and sashimi, and in 1972 the price reached $1.45 per pound. In 2001, a headless 440-pounder sold for $173,600.*

However, on days without fish, of which "we had hundreds," he was forced to make somewhat bitter runs to the mainland for fuel and ice with nothing to sell.

Further downeast, lobsterman and wildlife artist Rick Alley of Little Cranberry Island, off Mt. Desert, remembers going for tuna with his father as a pastime in the 1950s and 60s. "We went for a high price of about five cents a pound, if there was market at all, and we never went farther than a couple of miles from the island," he remembers. "Bakers Island, Bunkers Ledge, the eastern side of Islesford, and even up Frenchman's Bay to Egg Rock, all these places would sometimes have fish." They still are around, and he sees a few each year, but they are further out and smaller than the tuna he remembers as a child.

Maine sportsfishermen have also been in on the action. The oldest tuna event in Maine is the Bailey's Island Fishing Tournament, begun in 1939 to bring tourists and sports fishermen to the region. From the 1950s to the 1970s the tournament was an annual favorite. Gerry York, an Orr's Island genealogist and installation specialist at Bath Iron Works, recalls the high point with some 36 fish on the dock at once, and another time with a boat arriving unable to slow down, as it would start taking on water due to a heavy load of nine fish.

The tournament fish were also part of the Japanese boom, and local boatbuilder David Hackett recalls how "as often as not, they used to end up putting the fish over the side of the pier, until one day in the 1970s two quiet Asian men showed up dressed in suits and driving a Mercedes, and they bought the fish, pulled out a saw, put on coveralls, cut off the heads and tails and carted them off in a refrigerated truck."

The Bailey's Island event has been joined in recent years by the six-year-old Sturdivant Island Tuna Tournament, also run out of Casco Bay, which had a 931-pound fish landed in 1999, and offers as much as $12,500 in prize money.

## KING OF THE TUNAS

The giant bluefin tuna is a remarkable and highly evolved oceanic dweller. It is epipelagic (inhabiting the upper layer of the water column) and oceanadromous (traveling across open oceans), and is capable as an adult of visiting both brackish bay and open marine waters ranging in temperature from 40 to nearly 80 degrees. The fish ranges from 70 degrees north to 40 degrees south, with a sub-population off South Africa. It can live up to 20 years, and is capable of crossing 5,000 miles of open ocean in under two months, migrating in search of food. Adults become sexually mature at around 250 pounds, and

can attain weights of over 1,400 pounds. These days along the Maine coast anything over 500 pounds is notable, and the larger tuna of recent years for the most part have not been above 700.

Not only can it move across the face of the waters at will, but it can also move vertically with ease, diving up to 3,000 feet.

Tuna are regarded as the exception to the rule that fishes are cold-blooded: they are able to maintain higher than ambient body temperatures, and have evolved an elaborate circulatory system that acts as a countercurrent heat exchanger, keeping heat in the body.

Bluefin can thus maintain relatively constant large-muscle temperatures, allowing greater expenditures of energy and thus greater speed. With retractable pectoral fins smoothing their shape, they can push their hydrodynamic, bullet-like bodies to speeds exceeding 30 knots, and can change direction in any plane in an instant, hurling their entire mass well free of the water if they choose. On the other end of the energy equation, they also have mammal-like warm stomachs, allowing for protein digestion in about one third the time as other cold-blooded fishes, and thus greatly increasing the amount of food that can be ingested in a given time.

During their summer visits to the Gulf of Maine, adult bluefin have insatiable appetites, and will consume about 10 per-

*Beneath the surface, tuna are supported by far more than their own mass in other fish.*

cent of their body weight per day in herring, mackerel, hake, bluefish and squid. For hydrodynamic efficiency, tuna have given up the gill plates of most other fish (which allow them to fan water through their gills) and thus must swim ceaselessly or die.

## MANAGEMENT

The bluefin's major spawning grounds were long believed to be only in areas in the Gulf of Mexico and the central Mediterranean, a belief that led to the east-west, two-stock, split population makeup theory that has been the basis of management. Recent studies, however, have shown evidence of spawning in parts of the open Atlantic, in the region of the warm waters of the Sargasso Sea, further complicating both our biologic understanding and our attempts at conservation management. While the jury is still out, and no bluefin has been caught in *flagrante delicto* in the open central Atlantic, it has become apparent that they have a few heretofore unperceived tricks up their fins.

It seems that the tuna are literally swimming circles around the old two-stock theory, which held that the tuna of the eastern Atlantic (in the Mediterranean, North Africa and along the European coast) did not mix much with the fish of the western Atlantic waters. Management groups have had to work overtime to reconcile regulations with new knowledge, but have not moved fast enough for some environmental groups like the National

Audubon Society's Living Oceans Campaign.

Management authority for the giant tuna has been delegated to the International Commission for the Conservation of Atlantic Tuna (ICCAT), based in Spain. This group compiles statistics, coordinates research, develops management recommendations and brings the various tuna-catching countries together. It relies on the member countries for approving the regulations, and, most importantly, for enforcement and monitoring. In the United States, this management body is the National Marine Fisheries Service (NMFS). According to its figures, spawning size bluefin (those 320 pounds and larger) in U.S waters were last at the level at which a sustainable population can be maintained in 1975, and the numbers of both adults and juveniles have declined dramatically since, standing today at about 15 percent of the recommended level.

Split authority between national and international groups has in some cases left the fox in charge of the henhouse. At best, it has resulted in a somewhat unrestricted international fishery. (One person interviewed for this article went so far as to claim facetiously that the acronym ICCAT really stands for the "International Conspiracy to Catch All the Tunas.")

Whoever is in charge, it is certain that populations and distributions of bluefin have changed and perhaps crashed, with many countries on both sides of the Atlantic experiencing declining numbers

in the water and reduced catches on the docks. Now, some scientists are saying that the Atlantic bluefin tuna is heading deeper into danger of extinction. At best, the current level of fishing is believed to be holding the population level, and some believe it may be resulting in further declines. At the heart of the debate on catches, stock sizes and international allocations is the central, unresolved issue of whether or not there is one stock or two, and what is the size of the total population.

In the Gulf of Maine there is no question that the abundance of large bluefin has declined considerably from recorded levels of the mid-1990s, but the picture, like anything with these stealthy and rapid fish, remains unclear. Some believe the decline in numbers along the Maine shore is connected with the availability of baitfish, or that the tuna may have simply followed the lunch wagon. Unfortunately, the lunch wagon may be parked in another country's yard.

## MI TUNA ES SU TUNA?

Dr. Molly Lutcavage, a senior scientist with the New England Aquarium, has been tracking giant bluefin with sophisticated, data-gathering "archival" tags for over ten years. Her work, along with the efforts of Dr. Barbara Block of the Tuna Research and Conservation Center of Stanford University, and others, has shown that tuna tagged off the coast of Maine, New Hampshire and Massachusetts travel to the

*Maine fishermen have specialized in harpooning, a game of stealth and skill.*

Bahamas, the North and central Atlantic and even to the Azores, crossing well over the political line separating the eastern and western stocks.

The mixing rate of the two stocks was until recently assumed by ICCAT to be three to four percent, but is now believed to be closer to 40 percent—a tremendous difference, considering that the eastern Atlantic fishermen take about 12 times more fish (out of a total quota of about 70 million pounds) than their western counterparts. This critical information, not surprisingly, has led to widespread calls for eastern Atlantic fishermen to limit their catches more than they do.

Dr. Lutcavage is no stranger to being an iconoclast when it comes to debunking federal tuna information; her first work in the Gulf of Maine was in the early 1990s when she surveyed surface schools of bluefin from the air. She observed more fish on the surface than the federal authorities believed existed in the entire region, information that also affected the yearly quota setting process.

Within the Gulf of Maine, and especially within the range of the Maine islands, Dr. Lutcavage is now working on a striking new theory. While she recognizes that numbers of tuna coming near the coast and islands have decreased, she has also noticed that the schools of fish have maintained or increased their appearances elsewhere, such as in the Gulf of St. Lawrence and the Nova Scotian shore. She is beginning to look at other possible reasons for this shift out of the Gulf of Maine, such as a reduction in the availability of

food for the voracious fish. She has supporters in the commercial fishery for this theory, including longtime tuna-chaser Lexi Krause of Monhegan.

Krause also believes that Atlantic tuna comprise one mixed stock, and states "that this country has done the most for conservation, with less quota, no illegal market to speak of and effective enforcement, while Europe and Africa have unregulated fishing and markets, with us on this side paying the price."

But while the unbalanced quota on a mixed stock is a major factor, the problem goes even deeper, he thinks, and has another cause closer to home: the tuna have been left nothing for lunch.

As an island resident and a fisherman, Lexi has long observed species of all types, and he has noted a reduction in both size and abundance of schools of herring, whiting, mackerel and menhaden.

"If you take all the herring away, there is nothing for the tuna to eat, and they can and will take themselves to the feed," Krause says. The ecology of the herring stock in the coastal Gulf has become the top issue for Krause and other members of the East Coast Tuna Fishermen's Association. "The long and short of it is that the mid-water trawl boats are breaking up the bait schools, and it affects everybody, including the party (groundfish charter fishing) boats, the whale watching boats and the tuna fishermen," he says. "Consider that the herring is the basis of the whole chain, and without it the predators will just move out."

As always in underwater science, the picture is murky. Dr. Lutcavage points out that the effect might not be human-caused at all, but rather the result of higher water temperatures, which have been up as much as four degrees centigrade over a large area in 2002.

This summer, as the waters again become comparatively warm and still and the shoals of forage fish slide back into Maine waters, the giant bluefin tuna will not be far behind. But chasing the tuna into the gulf will be specters of their own: not just local harpooners and hookers pursuing the fish, but the larger twin shadows of deprivation of food through environmental alteration and the ceaseless stress of directed fishing pressure. They may be the fastest fish in the sea, but the tuna could still have a tough race staying ahead of these two tireless chasers. All who have enjoyed a slice of their violet meat, or have marveled at their tremendous proportions on the dock, or—best of all—seen one of these giants shooting improbably from the water, or who just like knowing that they are out there, should see in the bluefin tuna the apogee of the marine ecosystem of the Gulf of Maine. Like the tip of an iceberg, they are supported under the surface by far more than their own mass in other fish. If the numbers at the top are to remain, then it is not only to the fish themselves, but also to these casts of thousands that conservation efforts must be directed.

***Ben Neal*** *is Program Officer for Marine Resources at the Island Institute.*

*From* Blueberries for Sal.

Illustrations from *Blueberries for Sal,* copyright 1948, 1976; from *One Morning in Maine,* copyright 1952, 1980 by Robert McCloskey. Used by permission of Viking Penguin, a division of Penguin Young Readers Group, a member of Penguin Group (USA) Inc., New York. All rights reserved.

# Make Way for McCloskeys!

## SAL AND JANE GREW UP, BUT A PART OF THEIR LIVES HAS STAYED THE SAME

*Sal and Jane today.*

### STEVE CARTWRIGHT

"Kuplink, Kuplank, Kuplunk." If you've read Blueberries for Sal, you know that's the sound of fresh-picked blueberries dropping into an empty tin pail.

Since their publication half a century ago, three generations of children have known *Blueberries for Sal, One Morning in Maine, Time of Wonder*—classics by Maine writer-illustrator Robert McCloskey.

Little Sal and baby Jane remain forever young in their father's books. In real life, of course, they grew up, just like the rest of us. And Sal and Jane McCloskey today believe we can make the world a bit better, and we'd better not rest too easy until we've done so.

"Sal's mother and sister Jane were waiting with a box of empty milk bottles to return to the store and a list of things to buy," the familiar story goes. No more glass bottles in Bucks Harbor, but Condon's Garage is still there.

One morning in Maine, late last fall, I found myself aboard a boat headed to the McCloskeys' island. Turns out I had been here before, as a small boy on a sailboat, but none of us remember that visit. I won't soon forget this trip. The air was warm, the sea calm.

I ask the sisters if the stories are true. Jane says, "I don't think the bears were true. Bob wrote that book—*Blueberries for Sal*—because Mom was pregnant with me and Sally was beginning to realize there was going to be an interloper, an intruder in her life, and she did not take a good view of it. So Bob wrote *Blueberries for Sal* to give Sal a gift, to make her feel special. And *One Morning in Maine*—we always picked up feathers on the beach and wished on them."

The girls did go for ice cream at nearby Bucks Harbor. The characters, such as the Condons, are all real people. The son of the Mr. Condon who fixed the McCloskey outboard in the story—and in real life—has taken over from his father.

Remembering the old-timers of her childhood, Jane says, "Their names are so beautiful, Ferd, Earl, Percy, Oscar." The Clifford family, including Ferd Clifford, is now in its third generation of caretaking the island.

Robert McCloskey liked the local banter and salty character of Bucks Harbor, but he was bashful. He could relax at his island retreat, a tiny world bounded by inscrutable sea. The few surprises of island life were predictable if not always welcome, like a change in the weather.

As we chuff out of Swain's Cove for the short trip to the island, things feel vaguely familiar. Maybe this happens through shared ages and experiences, the common ground of hopes and disappointments, a shared need for even a small adventure, a fresh encounter.

Sal and Jane feel strongly about the Deer Isle region and its natural environment, and currently they are immersed in a battle to block salmon farming around the island that inspired McCloskey's classics, an area remarkably unchanged since.

We cruise around the bay to see the proposed salmon pen sites. We pass close by a seal, apparently playing with a floating log. We agreed we'd never seen that before.

"'I have a loose tooth!' Sal said to the seal, and the seal, being just as curious as most seals, swam nearer to have a good look."

The seal, I suppose, has often seen Sal and Jane before. He dives into the waters where the sisters hope they can fight off the salmon farm. They fear it will contaminate the marine ecosystem, threaten traditional lobster fishing and generally throw the balance of nature out of whack. Fighting for the environment—and the people —of the bay is something that brings the sisters—and their neighbors—closer, a common commitment.

Growing up in the shadow of Robert McCloskey meant, "Oh, you're Little Sal," "you're that Jane reaching for the ice cream cone" or clutching the spark plug on the way to "clam chowder for lunch."

It has been important to Jane and Sal to find themselves, and be themselves, apart from a certain celebrity status. It hasn't been easy. Both sisters have been married and divorced. Sal is remarried; Jane is single.

We walk along a narrow road on Little Deer Isle, picking wild apples. The sisters have some lines in their faces that betray hardships. Those lines can smile, too.

Says Jane, "I feel that I have finally come 'round full-circle to a happiness that I knew as a child and lost for so many years."

Sal acknowledges her own bumpy road, but has found comfort in a new relationship with her husband, Rod Chadbourne, a surveyor who moved from southern Maine, courting her gently with flowers and dinner.

"My view of the books is that they were great stories, which came out of our life on the island," she says. "They weren't necessarily about who we were or are as people, or how we personally experienced the events about which Bob wrote." But, she says, "they are wonderful stories."

Reaching the darkly wooded island, Sal and Jane adeptly bring their boat up to the sturdy dock, beside the boathouse where Robert McCloskey maintained a studio. We follow the worn path to the house.

Islands are always a little adventure. This one is hallowed ground, the place of stories. But change comes even to a well-preserved, family-owned island. The McCloskey house is undergoing a very thorough remodeling, and this is a last chance to glimpse the way it was.

Sal and Jane's small bedrooms upstairs are unchanged from their girlhood; so is the master bedroom with its portraits of the young sisters by their father. A computer looks out of place; one sister says it was their father's; the other sister says no, he never had his computer on the island.

*From* One Morning in Maine.

Photograph courtesy of Time Life

Life *Magazine visited the McCloskeys on the island in the 1950s.*

Robert McCloskey hasn't written a book in decades. He liked to invent things, to tinker. So he made elaborate mechanical puppets. "He never talked about them much," says Jane. "There were three puppets and they were going to be friends. Let me see, there was a mouse, a mole and pigeon. They hung out at the back of the school bus. The only one he ever really perfected was the mole. He ended up obsessing on the mole. He spent 20 years on it. The mouse was too small. The pigeon he was going to get to, someday, but the anatomy was screwy. How do you do the wings?"

He did some painting in those years.

The McCloskey portraits of his daughters draw your eye. The likeness to their faces today is remarkable, wondrous. Some things don't change. Some do. Downstairs, the big, two-story stone chimney in the house is gone—salt in the island sand used for mortar drew moisture into the chimney, weakening it. In the winter the moisture froze. Without the chimney, there is more view of the bay from the old couch where the girls snuggled with their mother, Peggy, as she read to them.

The old kitchen where Mom put up blueberries in glass-lid canning jars—while

Sal put the rubber rings around her arm— is being transformed. And that, the sisters admit, is a bit of a loss. But the house hadn't been kept up. The sisters agreed that it needed renovation.

When I was a child and later, when my children were young, *One Morning in Maine* and *Blueberries For Sal* were required reading, along with the McCloskey masterpiece, *Make Way for Ducklings*. At home, when I locate our dog-eared copies, son Joel, 18, glances at *Blueberries for Sal* and said, "Hey, leave that out. I want to read it." Never too old.

*From* One Morning in Maine.

On a window ledge in the island house is a model of the bronze statue of Mrs. Mallard and her Ducklings. The full size work sits on the Boston Common, site of the *Make Way for Ducklings* story—a mix of reality and make-believe. Another bronze of the ducks was installed in Moscow about ten years ago, and McCloskey was on hand for the event.

Not all McCloskey writing is Maine-based, but his beloved Scott Islands—there are two, just one with a house—run deep in his work. McCloskey's Maine is a place we recognize, superficially but also the undercurrents. The way children are loved, the understanding of natural environment, the quiet joys of small things. Every detail in a McCloskey picture counts—the rocks, seaweed, trees, stumps, clam hod, skiff, even the humor in Oscar Staples' face as Sal shows him where she lost a tooth.

McCloskey once said writing books was sort of an accident; he needed words to connect his pictures, and pretty soon he had a text. Part of the delight in these books stems from the stories being fiction, not life the way it really was, or is. Yet the stories ring true, free of cuteness or condescension. For McCloskey, the world of seals and his daughters at play on their island was irresistible material from which to craft a story. An indifferent, sometimes harsh world beyond the family and their island does not intrude.

Still, real things happen in those books, good and bad. Sal loses her loose tooth, and can't put it under her pillow. The outboard motor coughs and sputters, and her father ends up rowing to Bucks Harbor. There is mutual respect, between a bear and little Sal, young Jane and a storekeeper, between a girl and a seal.

Sal and her father now own the island. Jane was given her parents' Deer Isle home, which she sold several years ago. Jane lives simply in a modest, owner-built house, making wreaths and working with Sal on their East Penobscot Bay Environmental Alliance, organizing opposition to fish farming. Sal is a real estate lawyer who works with land trusts and other environmental groups.

Robert McCloskey, now 88 and widowed since 1991, bought a condominium at Parker Ridge, an assisted living facility in Blue Hill. He told me over the phone that he still wants to visit the island, but it's become difficult for him because of Parkinson's disease. I asked if I could visit him and he said he guessed not, that he was too old for interviews.

Bob McCloskey has memories he can lean on. In his books he evokes the essence of childhood and coastal Maine, and the not-so-easy but very worthwhile job of growing up. He has helped a lot of us grow, and appreciate what's around us.

*The* Life *photographs portray an idealized childhood.*

"When I was young I surrounded myself with musical instruments and tried the musician's life," McCloskey wrote in 1951. "Then I worked for hours with motors and wires and tried the inventor's life. With paints and brushes and such I have lived the artist's life. But you know, living on sea, I have been spending a lot of time with sea gulls and fish lately. Just this morning while I was shaving, I noticed a very slight difference in my whiskers. I examined them carefully but it is too early to tell whether they are changing into scales or feathers."

In *Time of Wonder*, the poetic book that is perhaps his most universal, he writes:

"Suddenly the wind whips the water into sharp, choppy waves. It tears off the sharp tops and slashes them into ribbons of smoky spray. And the rain comes slamming down."

"The moon comes out, making a rainbow in the salt spray, a promise that the storm will soon be over."

The next day, a McCloskey painting shows mother and father using a two-man crosscut saw to buck up downed trees. Sal and Jane find shells left by Indians, lying where the uprooted tree has exposed a layer of history.

Summer ends—we know that feeling. "Take a farewell look at the waves and the sky. Take a farewell sniff of the salty sea. A little bit sad about the place you are leaving, a little bit glad about the place you are going."

Sal and Jane have come back to the place where the story began, and they are finding their own rainbow in the salt spray.

---

**Steve Cartwright** *is a Maine-based freelance writer.*

*From* One Morning in Maine.

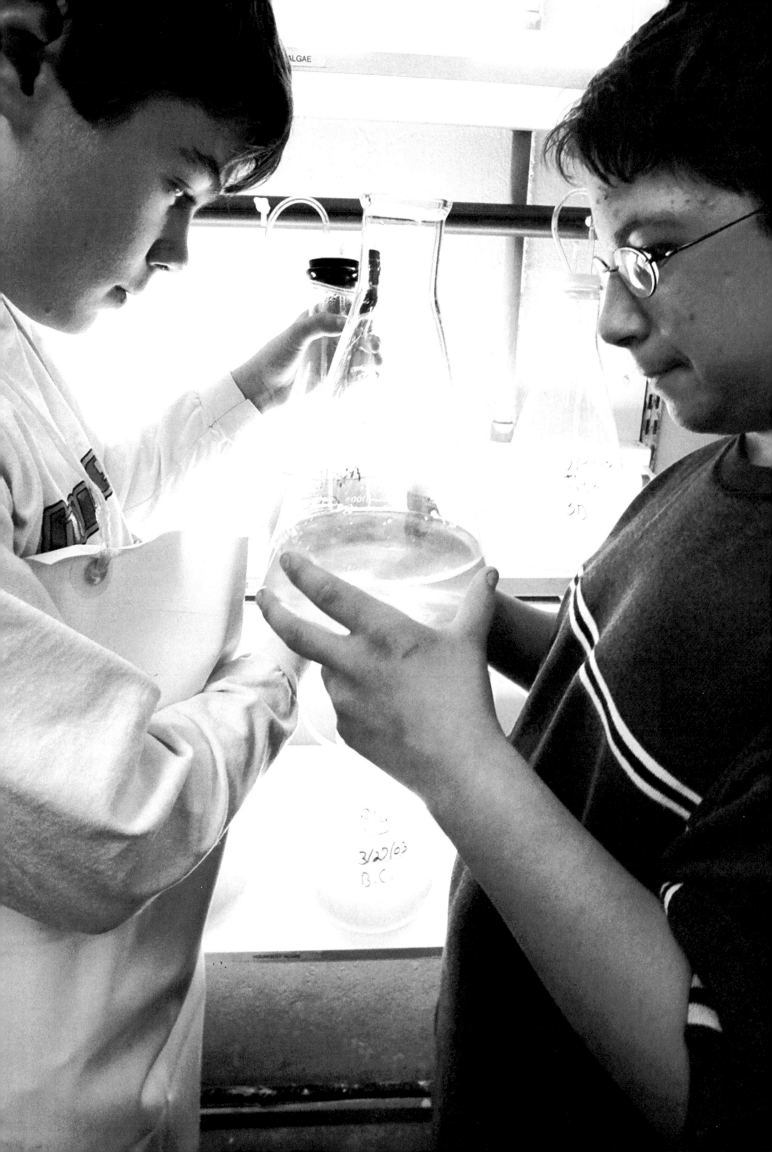

# Herring Gut

*At a seaside learning center, students raise oysters and expectations*

Peter Ralston (5)

STEVE CARTWRIGHT

At the tip of the St. George peninsula lies the snug village of Port Clyde, home to fishermen, artists and the Monhegan Boat Line. It's also the site of an unusual school, the Herring Gut Learning Center. A new building with attached greenhouse looks like a traditional Maine cape. But inside are labs with microscopes, fish tanks, classrooms and kids busily moving about and taking responsibility for different parts of the fresh water and salt water operations.

The Herring Gut Learning Center was founded five years ago by Phyllis Wyeth. The mission of Herring Gut—before Port Clyde, that was the name of this fishing village—is to introduce aquaculture and ecology to mid-coast middle and high school students and hopefully inspire them to further study, and possibly to careers in aquaculture.

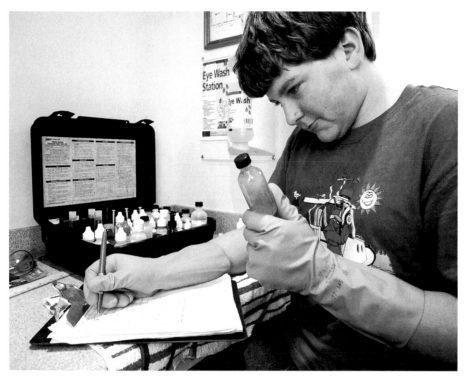

*Herring Gut introduces aquaculture and ecology to midcoast middle and high school students, hopefully inspiring them to further study.*

Eighth-grader James Lewis, son of a Cushing lobsterman, is one of the many students excited to attend Herring Gut. "In regular school, I just sat there being bored," he said. "Basically this place has given me a new life. I have more knowledge than I thought and I have more interest than I thought."

As Lewis attends to his duties as the Oyster Hatchery Manager—each

*Herring Gut emphasizes hands-on learning as the key for reaching students who have fared poorly in structured school settings.*

of the nine students in this alternate education program has a title and individualized responsibilities—he adds, "I'm going to try to get into marine biology when I get to college."

"At the beginning, we didn't think we'd get most of these students into high school," pointed out Jeff Chase, the Center's director. "Now they're talking about college." He hopes to see the center's reach extended beyond schools already served in St. George, Thomaston and Camden. "If nothing else," he said, "it sparks their interest in the marine sciences."

These kids aren't just learning marine biology. They learn to help each other in a business with a real budget, a real product. It's an experience that immerses them in work that is more than theoretical. Herring Gut emphasizes hands-on learning as the key for reaching these students who have fared poorly in structured school settings.

The Center is divided between two buildings including an oyster production facility below the new classrooms, greenhouse and lab facilities above. James Lewis shows us around the oyster facility and introduces us to 14-year-old Andrew Davis, president.

The operation is set up as a mini-business, and students keep track of expenses and the revenue they receive when they sell the oyster seed to growers.

When asked about his duties as president, Davis succinctly explains, "I have to make sure the meetings run well. I have to find weak spots in the company. I have to make sure the weekly reports get done. If someone is not doing the reports, there are consequences."

Clearly this approach to education has paid off for Davis. "Last year I flunked every subject in regular school. But this last quarter I was on the honor roll."

Sebastian Belle, executive director of the Hallowell-based Maine Aquaculture Association, has worked with Herring Gut for more than three years and is convinced of its importance. With the decline of the fishery, "young people from fishing families see no hope," he said. "They see mansions on the shore where they can mow lawns." Aquaculture, he believes, can change that.

"Herring Gut is in many ways re-igniting interest in the fishing industry," Belle said. "The center is teaching that the ocean has limited resources, and we exceed them at our peril. The center could provide careers on the Maine coast for the next generation of fishermen. Phyllis Wyeth wants them to have that chance."

About 200 students participate annually, including many who take part in a busy summer program. Chase has one paid assistant; another will be hired and volunteers round out the staff. This year they have expanded to offer a course and training for the "Zenith" alternative education program in Camden and have begun exploring a relationship with Rockland's alternative education program.

Wyeth often visits the center in her wheelchair, mingling with students and teachers and sharing their pride in new skills and discoveries, accomplished through their own hands-on efforts. Some of the students at Herring Gut are coping with various disabilities, and other difficulties at school and home. But for Wyeth, the center is really about possibilities. It's about cooperative learning and growth, about building self-confidence, making decisions, taking responsibility.

So far, it seems to be working.

Herring Gut flows from Phyllis Wyeth's own strong feelings about protecting the natural environment and the ocean's resources. That commitment extends to those who work the sea for a living, too.

By understanding how to grow algae to feed seed oysters, by understanding how oysters breed and develop, these young people "are learning all the skills," she said. "What's going to happen in a hundred years? We'd better prepare." Wyeth has for years been a director of the Natural Resources Defense

*The Center includes an oyster production facility, classrooms, lab facilities and a greenhouse.*

Council. She and artist-husband Jamie lived for years on Monhegan, where they literally watched the fishery decline. Now, many of the children who participate at the learning center are from local fishing families.

The new learning center building overlooks a quiet cove. Down the hill is Marshall Point Sea Farm, another Wyeth project. Sea Farm director Karl Eschholz said the business and the school programs go hand in hand; he is happy to help children learn the ropes, right down to the sex lives of oysters. He and Chase both studied biology at Unity College before signing on with Herring Gut.

The Sea Farm has sold market-size surf clams to Rockland's Cafe Miranda and Black Bull grill. But the biggest part of the business is seed oysters: 110 million raised and sold in 2001. Orders range in size from 100,000 to 20 million oysters. Students have to reckon with these figures, and Eschholz said, "I've never seen kids so excited about math." The center welcomes visitors, and can be reached by calling 207-372-8677. E mail: hglc@gwi.net

***Steve Cartwright*** *is a Maine-based freelance writer.*

*"Last year I flunked every subject in regular school. But this last quarter I was on the honor roll."*

# THE WORKING WATERFRONT

A quarterly newspaper
April 1993

# Despite everyone's best efforts, the worst could happen here

**By Christine Kukka**

Encased in a single skin of steel, nearly nine billion gallons of oil churns through the Gulf of Maine each year, passing near shellfish beds, rich fishing waters, national parks, commercial waterfronts, and visiting tourists.

Despite inch-thick spill response plans and millions of dollars spent on oil skimmers, booms, absorbent pads, and trained personnel from Portsmouth, N.H., to Eastport, the impossible-to-predict human or mechanical error could occur here.

It happened in Prince William Sound in Alaska three years ago. It happened in the Shetland Islands last winter. The contingency plans were in place, but they didn't prevent massive spills.

And once a spill occurs, despite recent technological advances in oil spill clean-up, there is still little that can be done to contain or clean it up, particularly on a coast like Maine's.

"I think it's fair to say we could be focusing more on prevention," said David Sait, who heads the oil spill response division at the Maine Department of Environmental Protection. "All the oil spill emergency

*(continued on page 11)*

## What we're up to...

This newspaper is a project of the Island Institute, a non-profit organization that got its start in Maine's year-round island communities. Island towns and their counterparts on the coastal mainland have much in common, and **The**

*(continued on page 6)*

## Inside

# THE WORKING
# WATERFRONT

### TURNS ·10·

DAVID D. PLATT

*David Platt,* Working Waterfront's *editor*

*Facing page:* Working Waterfront's *first issue considered the dangers of oil spills and recent rules designed to reduce them.*

L ate in 1992 at the Island Institute's old offices on Ocean Street in Rockland, an informal group began planning a new publication. The Institute's first newspaper, *Island News,* had already become *Inter-Island News,* a post office staple in the 14 year-round island communities and a forum for lively discussions of ferry service, solid waste and community life, along with a generous dose of "us vs. them" letters-to-the-editor.

The meetings that took place that winter were focused on something entirely different: a newspaper of broader interest, greater reach and more mainland potential than *Inter-Island News;* a journalistic enterprise that would be of interest, we hoped, to anyone who depended on the "working" waterfront to earn his or her living. The health of such places along the Maine coast—and their dwindling extent, due to development and gentrification—had been documented in early editions of *Island Journal* and had even been the object of a study by the State Planning Office. (The study's most startling finding: the number of miles of working waterfront on Maine's coast in the early 1990s was less than 25, and dropping.)

*Charlie Oldham has been* Working Waterfront's *designer since 1995.*

*Working Waterfront* was actually part of a larger effort to set up a marine resources program at the Institute. Philip Conkling (who chaired the aforementioned planning meetings) notes that this initiative was made possible through the generosity of the Birch Cove Foundation, which made resources available to the Institute after an unsuccessful effort to contribute to an island acquisition effort by The Nature Conservancy. "I'm sorry, sir," someone there had told Birch Cove's principal donor when he offered to "buy" a few petrel burrows in support of The Conservancy's apparently too successful island-saving fundraiser, "but the burrows are all sold." The donor switched allegiance to the Institute and its marine resources project, and the rest is history.

The early 1990s were a good time for new publications. Desktop computers, moderate paper prices and competition among job printers had made it possible for a single individual, or at least a very small number of people, to write, edit, lay out, print and distribute a newspaper at reasonable cost. If you could sell enough advertising, you could recoup some or all of your costs. In the case of nonprofit groups, a little-known fact even helped keep the postal rates down: in 1993, at least, the largest nonprofit bulk mailer in the country was the Catholic Church. Will Congress raise the rates or won't it? Go figure...

The name of the publication, it was decided, would be *Working Waterfront.* Like *Island Journal* (but unlike *Inter-Island News*), it would make use of coastal Maine's ample pool of freelance writers, photographers and graphic artists to fill its pages. For starters, at least, the editor

would design the paper himself on a computer, using the PageMaker program. It would appear quarterly, then six times a year, alternating with *Inter-Island News.* Thinking big, we decided to mail it to every box holder on a list of coastal and island towns, selected because they had working harbors or because a significant number of licensed working fishermen lived there. All Institute members would get the paper, as would others on a mailing list that included decision-makers and others with an interest in the coast. The press run for the first issue added up to over 20,000 copies—bigger than any other "alternative" paper in the state at the time, very big for a little place like the Island Institute; very new and adventurous for a publisher accustomed to high-end work like the *Island Journal* or a little community paper like *Inter-Island News.*

What to cover? Jump-starting a newspaper is harder than it looks. We went in search of stories that might lead us to other stories: the risks of oil spills, growing nori, a profile of a Portland wharf. We sought out op-ed pieces, looked around for interesting people to profile. We made a practice, in those early issues, of building each paper on a theme: old buildings with possibilities, small-scale aquaculture, the land-sea connection, finance, real estate, the promises of politicians. We also went looking for advertisers: marine contrac-

tors, gear suppliers, small manufacturers, folks with marine-related property to sell. Building an advertising base that would support a reasonable portion of our costs (this is a nonprofit enterprise) took about a year. Since 1994 we have tried, mostly successfully, to keep the "paid" portion of the paper at about 30 percent of the total space.

Ed Myers made his first appearance in September 1993, with a column called "All at Sea." He dissed a few lawyers, waxed eloquent about an aspect of aquaculture and entertained us with statistics. It marked the beginning of a relationship that lasted until his death nine years and 40 columns later. Roger Duncan followed, writing about the region's history. Rusty Warren and Phil Crossman signed on as island-based commentators. Ted Spurling had

Mike Herbert, ad sales and circulation.

been writing for *Inter-Island News* and continued there until we merged the two newspapers in 1996. He now writes a piece every other month, as do the other columnists.

Good writing has been at the heart of *Working Waterfront's* success. From the start we drew on the talents of experienced freelance writers: Christine Kukka, Francie King, Bob Moore, Bob Gustafson, Muriel Hendrix, Sandra Dinsmore, Bonnie Oldham and others. Institute staff members, particularly Philip Conkling and Ben Neal, have made major contributions, and a new generation of Island Institute Fellows now produces a steady stream of stories. After the first few issues, responsibility for the paper's design and production passed from the editor to a professional, first Anne Parrent, then the indefatigable Charlie Oldham. Anne (and before her, Sharon Smalley) sold ads between issues; then came Sandra Smith, followed by today's real pro, Mike Herbert.

The paper's mix of island and coastal news, business stories, profiles, history, commentary, letters, reviews, marine science and fishermen's wisdom seemed to work. Circulation reached 50,000 two years ago (we cut it back to just over 40,000 last year as the recession pushed ad revenues down, but we're still one of Maine's largest newspapers). We inaugurated a web edition, www.workingwaterfront.com.

The public response to the paper has been overwhelmingly positive since the beginning. Last winter a survey of the Institute's programs gave *Working Waterfront* high ratings, along with the Institute's Fellows program. The lessons of all this: start small, stay relatively modest, publish as frequently as you can afford, pay attention to your supporters and advertisers, listen to your writers and your readers, stay focused on the topics you have set out to cover, don't be afraid to try the unexpected. In our case the topics—the communities, economies and people of the coast of Maine—are of more than passing interest to a wide audience. Ten years into this project, we're feeling pretty good about it.

***David D. Platt*** *is editor of* Island Journal *and* Working Waterfront.

# "Howdja find New York?"

## *"We found it all right, just went straight down I-95"*

Nick McClellan, courtesy of the Bangor Daily News (2)

*Foy Brown enthralls the media outside the New Victory Theater.*

## *Maine Isle Takes Risk, Is Toast of Gotham*

LISA SHIELDS

Manhattan: 26 square miles; North Haven: 20.7 square miles. Not far apart, statistically, but what enormously different cultures. Both are islands in a technical sense, but how could city people possibly understand some of the narrative and lyrics that were so specific to our island community? New Yorkers, after all, had just endured an unimaginable injustice. Yet, despite—or perhaps because of—the horrors of Sept. 11, 2001, Manhattanites were entreating us to continue with our plans to perform the musical "Islands" at the New Victory Theater less than three weeks after the event.

"Islands" Director John Wulp, whose tenacity and ability to turn dreams into reality should never be underestimated, had arranged for the New Victory Theater lease and had prompted us to seek sponsorships both tangible and intangible. His sheer will seemed to preclude any thoughts to cancel our plans. Still, the prospect of New York, especially given recent events, seemed like far-fetched fiction.

*On stage in New York. That's Foy Brown on the screen in the background.*

Our New York date was Sept. 29; we were due to leave on the 28th. It seemed so soon after the raw wound, and some students and parents expressed concern about the appropriateness of the event, fears concerning safety and how far-ranging the physical manifestations of the devastation were. A meeting was held at the school to discuss the trip; it was decided to seek postponement. Then we learned, in the next few days, that the New Victory Theater, a performing arts theater for youth and family audiences, was essentially booked for a year. A subsequent meeting was held with the explicit intention of allowing respectful listening to all expressions of issues, opinions and concerns. By that time, many had received letters, phone calls and e-mails from friends in New York urging us to come. Still, some of us felt that we could be in the way of rescue and/or cleanup efforts. Others still had very real concerns about their families. The discussion was open and honest, and even some of us who still wanted to go felt it presumptuous that we could possibly bring any particle of solace to such devastation. Yet, as one cast member put it, "we might be putting a tiny band-aid on a gaping wound, but let's do it."

At the end of the meeting, a large majority voted to continue with the trip as planned. The final full rehearsal before taking off for New York was open to the public, with slightly over $1,100 in donations going to New York and Washington relief funds.

The media had muckled on to this story: tiny island community brings its message of community to an injured New York. So our arrival at the New Victory Theater on the afternoon of Sept. 29 was a news event. Cameras flashed as we exited our bus; video cams came at us from assorted directions; reporters' notebooks were at the ready and a stunned gathering of bystanders almost perceptibly ran brain scans to try to fit names to the 50-plus faces streaming off the bus. Some asked for autographs, perhaps thinking that a visible reminder would give them a hint as to what all this attention was about. It didn't—as one cast member kept saying, "but it's just us!"

A bad technical rehearsal in the afternoon left us drained and wondering what on earth we thought we were doing. Television crews remained outside the security-tight building (the cast and crew were required to wear badges) interviewing various cast members. Foy Brown, who was making a special appearance as himself for the "Joy of Foy" number, remained outside as theater personnel scrambled to find another badge for his wife, Viola. As a sound bite Foy was irresistible. "We found it all right, just went straight down I-95," he responded when asked how he found New York. Had we known the humor was outside the theater, we probably would have bagged the performance and all jumped ship.

Our call was 7 p.m. for an 8 p.m. performance. Musical director Aaron Robinson jump-started the cast and crew during warm-ups. His reassurance, and John Wulp's, bolstered our courage, though some of it leaked away again while we waited in the dressing rooms. The dressing rooms were actually equipped with make-up lights, lots of counter space and chairs, toilets, showers, ironing boards and irons, plugs for hair-dryers—a world away from the storage bays at the gym on North Haven where all our previous full performances had taken place.

When we got in line to go onstage at the New Victory Theater, most of us were in a bemused state; an aura of unreality permeated the atmosphere, and the enforced backstage quiet was effortless. Once again, there was the thought, "what on earth are we doing here?"

It all became obvious as we filed onstage. The clapping began, and grew in intensity and volume as more of us entered. Then the cheering began, and row by row the 500 people in the audience stood up to greet us. The love and support that flowed from them almost overwhelmed us, and many of us, particularly the adults, wondered how we would sing with lumps in our throats and tears in our eyes. We stood on that stage, transfixed at the welcome, but grinning from ear to ear. The current of support and affection that flowed back and forth between that audience and that stage was palpable…

*Lisa Shields is a longtime resident of North Haven, a member of the "Islands" cast and a former Community Service Director at the Island Institute.*

Hello. I'm David Cooper.

Except for the three years I spent in the Army stationed in Berlin, I've lived on North Haven all my life. And there were eight generations of Coopers here before me. I've done just about everything you can to make a living on this island, from digging clams to hauling for lobsters. Fifteen years ago I hurt my back and since then I've worked as the rural mail carrier. This has given me the opportunity to talk with just about everyone on this island, so there isn't much going on here that I don't know about. Nothing very exciting ever happens on the island, but whatever does happen seems somehow more intense, heightened. This is a great place to bring up kids. My grandchildren can't imagine living anywhere else. And I suppose it's some sort of recommendation that people who have lived here all their lives want to be buried here. Only the teenagers want to get away. Perhaps that's only natural. Most of them come back…eventually.

*Everybody looks,*
*everybody sees,*
*everybody hears,*
*everybody knows;*
*What everybody says,*
*what everybody does*
*What everybody thinks,*
*where everybody goes.*

*Every single day, everything we do*
*Actually depends on the way the wind*
*blows*
*On this island.*
*We belong here*
*On this island…*

# "*Approximately My*

## NORTH HAVEN

### IN MEMORIAM: ROBERT LOWELL

*I can make out the rigging of a schooner*
*a mile off; I can count*
*the new cones on the spruce. It is so still*
*the pale bay wears a milky skin, the sky*
*no clouds, except for one long, carded, horse's-tail.*

The islands haven't shifted since last summer,
even if I like to pretend they have
—drifting, in a dreamy sort of way,
a little north, a little south or sidewise,
and that they're free within the blue frontiers of bay.

This month, our favorite one is full of flowers:
Buttercups, Red Clover, Purple Vetch,
Hawkweed still burning, Daisies pied, Eyebright,
the Fragrant Bedstraw's incandescent stars,
and more, returned, to paint the meadows with delight.

The Goldfinches are back, or others like them,
and the White-throated Sparrow's five-note song,
pleading and pleading, brings tears to the eyes.
Nature repeats herself, or almost does:
*repeat, repeat, repeat; revise, revise, revise.*

Years ago, you told me it was here
(in 1932?) you first "discovered *girls*"
and learned to sail, and learned to kiss.
You had "such fun", you said, that classic summer.
("Fun"—it always seemed to leave you at a loss...)

You left North Haven, anchored in its rock,
afloat in mystic blue...And now—you've left
for good. You can't derange, or re-arrange,
your poems again. (But the Sparrows can their song.)
The words won't change again. Sad friend, you cannot change.

ELIZABETH BISHOP

### CARL LITTLE

W hen the poet Elizabeth Bishop's letters were published in 1994, a nearly 700-page volume titled *One Art*, the reviewers spent much of their allotted space highlighting the dark side of her life as revealed in her correspondence. There were Bishop's bouts with alcoholism, her troubled relationships and periods of illness. As she remarked later in life, "Being a poet is one of the unhealthier jobs."

It was the rare critic who mentioned Bishop's trips to Maine, for the most part relaxed and pleasurable times, from the earliest visits to Wiscasset and Stonington in 1948 to the final summers spent on North Haven in the 1970s. Maine served Bishop, as it has so many writers and artists, as a refuge—a land, to play on a line of Robert Lewis Stevenson, of counterpain.

Bishop (1911-1979) was a keen observer of life. Her attention to detail led to some of the finest poetry of the 20th century. "Roosters," "The Prodigal," "The Fish," "One Art," "In the Waiting Room"—these and many other poems appear in nearly every anthology of American verse. When her last book, *Geography III*, came out in 1976, poet Anthony Hecht wrote that Bishop's new work "was about the finest product our country can offer the world... It beats our cars and films and soft drinks hollow."

*A limited edition broadside of "North Haven,"*
*printed in 1979, is illustrated with a drawing*
*by British artist Kit Barker, a friend of Elizabeth*
*Bishop's. Courtesy of Carl Little*

# Idea of Heaven"

## ELIZABETH BISHOP ON NORTH HAVEN

The letters provide further demonstration of Bishop's observant eye. Those sent from Maine are filled with descriptions of the landscape and the inhabitants. In a letter from early September 1948, she offered her friend and fellow poet Robert Lowell a few vivid impressions of Stonington:

*The boats bringing the men back from the quarries look like convict ships & I've just been indulging myself in a nightmare of finding a gasping mermaid under one of these exposed docks—you know, trying to tear the mussels off the piles for something to eat—horrors.*

In 1974 Bishop started spending a part of each summer on North Haven. On July 30 of that year, she sent a postcard view of the island to friends. She was clearly smitten by the place: "This is the village—one general store—the rest is fields and woods, very much like Nova Scotia—and birds & wildflowers. Alas, we have to go back in a few days."

The island, "which is approximately my idea of heaven," Bishop wrote a friend in July 1975, provided a splendid respite from teaching duties at Harvard and elsewhere. The poet stayed at Sabine Farm, so called, she states in one letter, "because Mrs. Pettit's husband's first name was Horace!" She entertained friends (as Lowell once said, "In Maine your friends pour in like lava—hot from their cities"), but also enjoyed the remoteness. "The few 'summer people' have mostly gone there for years & years, are all fearfully rich, dress in rags, and the houses are far apart," she wrote in August 1975. "I can't see another one from 'Sabine'—just fields down to the water, fir trees, wildflowers, and a vast view of Penobscot Bay, islands, schooners, and so on-and it is silent, except for bird songs."

Apropos birds, in a letter from June 21, 1977, Bishop recounted an all-day Audubon Society trip to see puffins. "It was really fun—and funny," she reported.

"We were supposed to see something called 'The Sooty Shearwater' (& did) & Alice [Methfessel] had promised to call out, 'Oh—there's a Shitty Sorewater!' She really did say this to our guide, but apparently he didn't notice anything & just said 'Where?' "

Bishop's letters from these years offer humorous tidbits from a summer Maine island. Writing to a friend on July 18, 1977, she mentioned a neighbor, Emily Lattimore, who told the poet that if she came to the island for 12 years she "might get invited to a cocktail party." In another letter Bishop referred to the island's "R.F.D. man," Colon Winslow. "He used to weigh 300 lbs. and since he now weighs only 200 he is called 'Semi-Colon.' "

Later that summer Bishop described a sail on a 40-foot sloop around North Haven and a trip by lobster boat to visit the visionary architect Buckminster Fuller. In a note to poet James Merrill she admitted "dreading leaving" North Haven to face a teaching stint at New York University. "My one desire is to retire," she related. "This is no doubt due to lack of vitamins or something—but tonight we have our last Maine lobsters—thrashing around in a bucket now."

A letter from the following year recounted the "hectic" nature of life on the summer island:

*And the "news" is scarcely lively: today we go to the "store," and—if we get there before two—we can go to the ladies' cake sale at the church. Also, we can go to buy some lettuce, etc., at a sort of farm a young girl and her husband are running this season. The last time we went there a very grande-dame-sort-of summer-resident, with large hat & basket, said to me, "Tomorrow we can probably buy green beans; won't that be fun?" So you see how hectic things are here.*

Bishop's last summer on North Haven appears to have been completely uneventful. "The only thing I can think of to say is 'I don't know where the summer's gone to,' " she wrote to a friend on August 30, 1979. "I think one of the reasons for the general indolence & forgetfulness," she remarked, "was that it was the foggiest summer ever on record. (One man said, 'No, '63 was a little worse.')" This "fogginess," she noted, "seems to make one sleepy, lazy, and extra-remote." These words seem prescient: Bishop died shortly after, on October 6, in her apartment in Boston.

To my knowledge, there is only one Bishop poem that refers directly to these Maine sojourns, but it happens to be a major one: "North Haven," her elegy to Robert Lowell. Since its publication in the complete edition of her verse (1983), the poem has become a part of the American literary canon.

A limited edition broadside of "North Haven" was printed in 1979, illustrated with a drawing by British artist Kit Barker, who had visited Bishop on the island in 1978. I count myself among the fortunate to own a copy of this broadside, signed by the poet. I stop to read it all the time, relishing the flow of words, especially the second stanza, which so beautifully renders the island landscape:

*The islands haven't shifted since last summer,*
*Even if I like to pretend they have*
*— drifting, in a dreamy sort of way,*
*a little north, a little south or sidewise,*
*and that they're free within the blue frontiers of bay.*

Had she lived longer, Bishop might have transformed more of her island experiences into poetry. As it is, we have "North Haven" and a marvelous group of letters to serve as testimony to her love for this part of Maine.

*Carl Little won the Friends of Acadia 2002 poetry contest with the poem "Ten Tourists Visit Baker's Island, ca. 1900." He is Director of Communications at the Maine Community Foundation.*

# Death, Life, & Rising Water

## On a Chesapeake island, the living and the dead share limited space

BRENDAN DONEGAN

Tangier, Virginia, is a teardrop-shaped island just south of the Maryland line in the lower reaches of the Chesapeake Bay. One of its notable features is the way graves are interspersed with the homes. The dead are laid to rest among the living here; on this low-slung spit of land, the residents compete with their departed ancestors for the scarce dry soil.

While some burials still occur on family lots, most islanders are now interred in the new church graveyard that lies just beside the playground of the island's combined elementary, middle and high school. On a bright February morning not long ago, one grave stood out. Red poinsettias and yellow Fuji chrysanthemums were heaped high on the disturbed earth where Becky Wheatley had been buried just three weeks before.

On Saturday, Jan. 18, 16-year-old Becky Wheatley, blond, five-foot-ten, with vivacious eyes, went ashore with her 24-year-old boyfriend to ride with him to Camp Lejeune in North Carolina. Her father told her in the morning that he didn't want her to go ashore that day; he didn't feel right about it. Becky insisted, and he finally relented.

They took the island's mailboat, the COURTNEY THOMAS, to Crisfield, Maryland, 11 miles away, and from there they drove south in her boyfriend's red Mercury Cougar. As they passed Chesapeake, Virginia, debris fell from a dump-truck onto the highway right in front of them. Her boyfriend swerved, but lost control and plowed into a tree. He survived, but Becky ended her short life 75 miles from her island home, crushed in a tangle of metal.

When word came back to Tangier, the whole community quickly learned of her family's sorrow. Returning watermen say they noticed a distinct pall over the island even before they came ashore. Becky's funeral service was held in Tangier's white clapboard Swain Methodist Church in the middle of the island. Some said that the only other funeral as sad in recent years in this close-knit community was when a young pregnant woman died and her unborn child succumbed a few minutes later. Islanders recalled seeing Becky walking around the island a few days before, the picture of health. Now she was lying before the altar, concealed in a coffin, gone forever. So young. The mournful sounds of the church bell tolling for her carried out over the bay waters to the few Tangier men who were tonging for oysters that day. Ninety extra chairs were brought in from the Sunday school next door to seat the crush of mourners, 600 at least, elbow-to-elbow.

Becky was put in the ground 30 yards from the church, just beside the narrow paved lane that leads to the school. Tears flowed hard when her distraught boyfriend laid his hand on her casket as it was lowered into the shallow concrete vault that is used for burial in this island's waterlogged soil. Three weeks later, two large plastic hearts still rattled in the wind above

her grave, sending a stark warning of the fragility of life to all who would pass by.

Tangier does not need more reminders of death. Graves are everywhere. There are burials in church graveyards, in family plots, in side, rear and front yards. Sometimes there are tombstones, often little ones for infants, only inches from front-door stoops. Over 20 separate burial grounds lie within a quarter-mile of the center of the community. On this eroding 950-acre island—it was losing twenty square feet each year until a seawall was built in 1990 to protect its airstrip—only 104 acres of dry land remain. Even the dry land is not so dry: dig a hole one or two feet down, and it quickly fills up with muddy water seeping in from all sides.

The usable land is perched amongst the marshes on three narrow sand ridges rising less than five feet above the surrounding waters. Main Ridge, the longest, is in the middle; Canton Ridge lies to the east and West Ridge overlooks the bay. Two wide swaths of musky saltmarsh meadows, laced with meandering tidal creeks and guts, separate the ridges. Two hundred and seventy-six homes—mostly white clapboard Tidewater Victorian houses, with a sprinkle of late-20th-century trailers—are tightly packed on postage-stamp lots, clustered like vertebrae along the ten-foot wide lanes that run north and south along the ridges. Narrow causeways with hump-backed wooden bridges cross the saltmarshes.

Seven hundred and twenty men, women and children live here. From a distance, their crisp houses look like survivors clinging to the keel of an upturned boat.

This windswept island, now barely three and a half miles long and one and a half miles wide, located twelve miles west of the Virginian Eastern Shore, is believed to have received its first European settlers in 1686—John Crockett and his eight sons. Legend has it that the Potomac Indians sold the island for two overcoats. Almost everyone on the island today is descended from these original settlers. Family names are repeated many times on the island's tombstones. On the monument to those who fought in World War II beside the church on Main Ridge, out of fewer than 100 names there are 27 Crocketts, three Charnocks,

seven Dizes, 22 Parks, 15 Pruitts, four Shores and five Wheatleys. Even those who don't carry these surnames are related. "There is a piece of Crockett and Pruitt in everyone," says Grace Brown, who runs a bed-and-breakfast on the island. One-third of the island's inhabitants now bear the Crockett surname.

Dewey Crockett was Becky's teacher. He is also the assistant school principal, mayor of Tangier, church organist, undertaker's helper, ambulance driver, occasional preacher and husband to the island's nurse. Becky was a junior. Her seat up front, fourth row in from the window in her map-shrouded classroom, stands starkly vacant. "No one else dares to sit there," said Crockett. "It is hard on the school children when they pass so close by her grave, when they play outside, or come and go from school."

He would have preferred that Becky's grave was located further away from the school grounds, but there was nowhere else to put it. The island is running out of burial space. The church cemetery is the only choice available for most islanders. Older residents don't want to be buried on the mainland. Whenever a house is abandoned, there is pressure to convert the site to another cemetery. The Daughters of America's Hall was demolished to provide the space near the church where Becky lies. Here the church elders decided that the departed should be laid out in the sequence that they die, in contrast to the more customary way of grouping by families.

This rule has put Becky right up against the waist-high Sears chain-link fence that separates the cemetery from the schoolyard. Mary Wheatley, 94, a distant relative who died earlier in the month, lies in a fresh grave at her feet, and Jack McCreedy, 76, who died after her, lies directly to her right. Walter Edward "Sonny" Parks, 67—he died of cancer—begins the next row, and Etta Parks, 91, follows. The grim reaper's January harvest is all nicely arranged chronologically. "You have to be careful not to make enemies on this island because you never know who will be buried beside you," said Grace Brown.

Wade Creedle, Jr., was Becky's pastor. "The whole island was paralyzed by Becky's death," he said. A burly man with a well-rounded belly crossed by black suspenders, he was called to give counseling to the schoolchildren to help them with their grief. "Ashore, the school system

*Ginny Marshall's roster of the island dead*

Brendan Donegan (3)

*Ginny Marshall, caretaker.*

brings in professional counselors to help the children cope when there is a sudden death like this, but on the island we could not bring outsiders. It wouldn't work," he said. "This is a very closed society here. Very proud."

Ginny Marshall recorded Becky's death on the inside of the cover of one of her four Bibles. At 76, she tells of being blinded in one eye as a teenager by a mote from the exhaust of her father's workboat, which put an end to her dream to go off to New York and become an opera singer. She still rides her bicycle to the post office every afternoon after the mailboat arrives. Sometimes, when there, she gets news of someone else who has passed away. In her Bibles she keeps a long list of all the deaths of persons who were born on Tangier, religiously adding the new names each month in her neat copperplate writing. This last January has kept Ginny particularly busy. During the month, six persons who lived on the island had died. An additional 12 persons, who were born on the island but had moved ashore, had also passed away. Usually only seven or eight people from Tangier die in a whole year. January was almost like old times—in the 19th century, successive epidemics of cholera, tuberculosis, measles and smallpox took a heavy winter toll.

Ginny is particularly troubled by Becky's untimely death. "They say it was her time. I can't believe that if she had heeded her father's advice and stayed home, she would have died that very day here on the island." she said. "If a waterman who couldn't swim fell overboard and drowned, would we say 'it was his time,' or would we say that it was his foolishness that brought on his early death?" Ginny, like most of the islanders, is a devout Methodist and has a strong belief in the

literal meaning of the Bible. "The Word says that 70 years is our appointed lot, and Becky only lived part of her allotted time."

Ginny knows where she will be buried when her own time comes. Standing on her tiptoes and looking out her kitchen window, she can see the family graveyard out back of her mother's house, just two doors south of the parsonage next door. Looking there brings to her mind the Great Storm of August 1933. A unique confluence of a Northeaster and a hurricane barreling in from the Atlantic, coupled with a new moon, drove the bay waters up five feet, inundating most of the island. Ginny was just six at the time. "It was in the morning. The tide kept getting higher. I was frightened. It came up to the second step on the stairs in my mother's house. Our grapevine and a pear tree were carried away. Big boats were afloat all over the island." Her departed grandfather's coffin popped up out of the ground in the family graveyard and floated about. When the tide receded later that day, neighbors retrieved her grandfather, pumped out his burial vault, put the coffin back in, replaced the lead seal and battened him down good and strong.

Coffins rose up from graves all over the island during that memorable storm. The frail brick-and-mortar covers arched over the vaults were no match for the force of the upwelling water. Today, burial vaults have massive stone or concrete lids that will keep the departed down should the waters rise again. Each weighs over 900 pounds and takes four strong men to lift. Like schools of grounded albino whales, these mounded half-round shapes, all painted white, nuzzle together in corners alongside the lanes and byways of Tangier.

Robert Bradshaw, Sr., was Becky's undertaker. When he recalled her funeral,

his solemn eyes stared forward as he sat in his office behind the perfumed viewing rooms in his funeral parlor in Crisfield. "There was something about it that I never experienced in all my years. During the service at the church, I went out three times to check on the grave site. Each time when I stepped outside, not a soul, nothing, neither a person, nor an animal, a motorcycle or a boat was moving, or even in sight. The whole island was utterly silent."

Tangier Island is usually a noisy place. The winds carry snatches of conversation across the marshes. There are the sounds of dogs barking, the sounds of children shrieking at after-school play, the sounds of boat engines roaring into life in Mailboat Harbor, the rattling of the odd pickup truck as it makes its way along the narrow lanes.

Bradshaw's grandfather started in the funeral business in 1896. He remembers when he was ten, in 1942, riding out to Tangier for the first time on his grandfather's white hearse-boat, KING TUT, to help him with a funeral. "Back then, the women wore sunbonnets and came to the funerals still wearing their aprons. Mostly women attended funerals. The younger men were away at war, and the older men were working out on the water." Funerals are different on the island now. As many men as women attend. "Tangier islanders are more emotional at funerals than those on the mainland," said Bradshaw. "They are very closely related, and when someone is taken away from them, especially suddenly, they all feel the tragedy. Their grief goes deep and wide."

Because the graves are so interspersed with the houses on Tangier, the islanders have no way to avoid passing them as they go about their daily lives. The graves are right there in front of the children as they play, as they bounce on trampolines and wander the lanes on their way to and from school. They are there as the watermen head to their boats before the morning's first light. They are there too as the women of Tangier step out of their houses and find their way to the island's two grocery stores, the church, the post office or the harbor. There is no hiding from the reality of death here. "We all know that we are eventually going to die," said Bradshaw. "However, I find on the mainland, that not everyone believes it."

On Tangier, amid so many reminders of mortality, it must be different.

**Brendan Donegan** *is a freelance writer based in Columbia, Maryland.*

# Goin' Down to the water

Story by
PHIL CROSSMAN

*Illustrations by*
JON LUOMA

Othney Phelps Birch has a singularly remarkable, some might say unfortunate, name. Beyond that, he dresses in a way that, here on the island, has the unhappy result of making him stand out like a pair of wingtips at the Swap Shop. An authoritative assessment suggested that the retail value of the wardrobe in which Phelps chose to appear at the January meeting of the Vinalhaven Planning Board exceeded, for example, the yearly cost to the town for the services of the Knox County Sheriff. And the fact that, superficially anyway, the impact of the wardrobe on Birch was more productive than the impact of the Sheriff on the people of Vinalhaven did not diminish the perception that Othney Phelps Birch might be a little stuck on himself. On the appointed evening he sat, amused and long-suffering, in a cold, folding metal chair, through what he clearly saw as a mundane discussion of the several equally tiresome items appearing on the agenda ahead of the one with which he was concerned. Already annoyed, he took note of the little white oven timer on the table in front of one board member, ticking loudly and incessantly as the proceedings dragged on. Assuming it was there to cut short long-winded applicants, he barely stifled a disdainful chortle at this brutish alternative to the Rules of Order. Eventually, about half an hour after the meeting got under way, Mr. Birch rose in response to the chair's recital of item 5, to wit: "Application of Douglas VanMiddlesworth to build a boathouse and dock on Lot 15 of Map 12."

Othney stood and gave the Board and the others in attendance a moment in which they might fully appreciate the humbling image of himself packaged in a Loro Piana Houndstooth jacket, Raffaello silk tie and Versace Algonquin evening shoes. "Madame Chairwoman and distinguished members of the board," he began, "I am Othney Phelps Birch, senior partner at Conan & Trumble, Cambridge, Massachusetts. I represent Douglas VanMiddlesworth, who is seated here at my left and on whose behalf I will speak in the unlikely event any of you have questions regarding this exceedingly ordinary application for a building permit. Also present tonight and seated at my right is Mr. VanMiddlesworth's architect, Brentley Sweet. I personally prepared this application for the Board's consideration following an extensive review of your Zoning Ordinance by my staff. Furthermore, I have gone the extra mile, as it were, to appear before you in person here tonight."

"Excuse me O.P.—don't mind if I call you Opee do ya?" interjected board member Louie Hopkins, who was seated farthest back from Mr. Birch. Before Opee had a chance to answer, Louie continued. "Ya know the little woman and me damn near picked up a jacket just like that one you got on, over to Reny's just 'fore Christmas. Hell of a buy it was but wicked tight, I couldn't quite get into it. We was thinkin' we might go down to the Damariscotta store next week when we go over to see her mother at the hospital, see if they got one there a little bigger. You happy with that one you got?"

His stride knocked momentarily askew, Opee allowed as how he was, indeed, happy with the jacket and as he instinctively released the two tethering buttons and spread the right and left sides with each hand so as to display the brocade and its raised silk lining better, he continued, "Thank you indeed for asking. Now, as I was saying—"

Louie didn't hesitate for an instant and, assuming that Opee, in opening his jacket, was offering it to him, he pushed his wooden armchair back, got to his feet and surged forward to receive the offering. Louie, when he reached Opee, turned 180 degrees in the manner of one who expected help getting into a jacket. Opee, fearing that to do otherwise would be to derail further the momentum of his presentation, had little choice but to remove it from his own torso and help it onto Louie's, whereupon Louie pirouetted around to offer his hand in gratitude and returned to his seat, comfortable not only with the gesture but with the fit.

A little desperate to regain the high ground he felt he'd secured, Opee continued, "Mr. VanMiddlesworth negotiated a purchase of the property in question, the former Ingerson homestead, on the east shore of Carver's Harbor, after an examination by my firm confirmed clear title and revealed no significant obstacles to his plans to expand the existing structure and to build an accessory guesthouse—forgive me, an accessory boathouse—and to improve the existing dock on the shore. I have here five complete and extensive plans each of which include elevation and footprint views of the various levels of the house and boathouse, schedules of materials and utilities, site preparation and landscaping plans." Opee retrieved the five scrolls from an assistant two seats down, a young man he'd ignored in his introductions, and ceremoniously presented them to each board member. Each package was

---

*"Now about this guesthouse; excuse me, boathouse," asked board member Cheryl Goodheart. "The plans call for a fireplace and entertainment center and frankly, that gives me pause."*

---

wrapped in a chartreuse silk ribbon. The five board members opened their sets of plans. Each three by four feet, the five sets consumed 60 square feet, significantly exceeding the 48 square feet of table space available. In the process a cup of hot coffee was overturned into the lap of Madame Chairwoman and, following a brief recess during which she regained her composure and cleaned herself up, the board reconvened. Opee, after repeatedly expressing his concern to the Chair, continued from where he'd left off.

"As you can see from the plans and accompanying material…"

The white timer suddenly sounded so furiously that it literally jumped around a little until board member Harriet Peterson tapped its little button and announced, "Excuse me everyone, time to tend to the cookies." Accordingly the Chair signaled another recess and Harriet threw on her coat and left. During the 15 minutes it took Harriet to complete her errand, the remaining three members admired and exclaimed over Louie's new jacket. He'd removed the ineffectual handkerchief Opee had tucked into the breast pocket and substituted his own oft-used plaid bandanna. The previous week's Uncle Henry, corseted in the right jacket pocket, challenged the fabric's structural integrity and promised a more comfortable fit for next week's issue. Before long Harriet returned with a plate of hot tollhouse cookies, some milk was retrieved from the fridge the firemen maintained in the corner of the meeting room, and milk and cookies were had all 'round before the meeting reconvened. The Chair asked Opee to remind everyone of where he'd left off, which he did. Redirecting their communal attention to the plans spread out before them, Opee again reminded them of the straightforward nature of this application and asked if he might expect a vote.

"Vote? Oh sure," replied the Chair, "just give us a minute to talk it over and see if anyone in the audience wants to speak to the issue." Opee sat down, not yet fed up with this unprofessional and primitive process and the emerging insubordination of the board members, but not far from it. He crossed his legs and patiently flicked a speck of cookie crumb from his knee.

"Now about this guesthouse; excuse me, boathouse," asked board member Cheryl Goodheart. "The plans call for a fireplace and entertainment center and frankly, that gives me pause. As you no doubt know, one strategic purpose of the zoning ordinance is to preserve shoreland, particularly in and around the harbor, for activities related to commercial fishing. How do you propose to demonstrate this water-dependent use required for approval?"

Opee snapped to his feet. "Good question, ma'am, very good indeed and I'm glad you asked it, very glad in fact. Mr. Vansmiddlesworth maintains a 35-foot Grand Banks Trawler. No doubt you are all aware of the historic maritime role played by this classic working boat. The importance of its contribution to the time-honored fishing tradition, so much a part of this island's own heritage, will live on in this noble craft whether it be bobbing proudly on its mooring out front or waiting out the winter in the anticipated boathouse." Opee sat down.

"So you're gonna' fish with that trawler, gonna be a fisherman are you, Doug? You don't mind if I call you Doug do ya?" queried Jeff Allenton. "That last name of yours is kinda time consumin'."

"Mr. VanMiddlesworth will—" began Opee, getting to his feet, but Jeff interrupted him.

"You can sit down, Opee. We want to hear from Doug himself. Applications like this are a lot easier to swallow if the proposed waterfront use is convincing. You plan on fishin' with that trawler, Doug?"

"I really must insist," answered Opee, rising again, "That I am representing—"

"Don't get your foot stuck in the gear there, Opee. We ain't in court and we can hear from Doug if we want to."

Doug answered with some hesitation, "Well, of course, once we get settled, I probably will, uh, I expect I'll, you know, kind of, like fish."

"Well that's a relief, gonna make this application a lot easier to deal with," sighed Grant Ames, a fisherman himself. "Just outta curiosity, Doug, what kind of fishin' do you expect to do with your trawler and where exactly?"

"Well I, uh, hadn't given it much thought, you know, thinking I'd decide once we'd moved in and got things figured out. What kind of fishing you ask? Well I expect I'll uh, I guess I'll, uh, you know, like trawl. Yes, that's it, of course. The boat's a trawler after all. I'll, like, trawl."

"And where 'bouts exactly?"

"Well, uh, I guess on the, you know, Grand Banks."

"I continue to be relieved," replied Grant. "Thanks."

"Now are there any questions or comments from the audience?" asked the Chair.

Muffin Peabody stuck his hand up. Muffin owned a fish house just to the south of Doug's property. "Go ahead, Muffin," acknowledged the Chair.

"Well, as you know, my boys and me live next door to this property but we got no water frontage. My family fishes off the Ingerson wharf, have for near a hundred years. Matter of fact the only way we can get to our fishhouse is to drive down Ingerson's driveway and across the sou'west corner of his lawn. The guesthouse he wants"—"Boathouse," interjected Opee—"is right in the driveway and completely blocks the only way to the wharf. Matter fact the only way to get to the wharf is gonna be through the guesthouse," finished Muffin.

"Boathouse," objected Opee. "If it please the court," offered Opee, standing,

"I was hoping this minor obstacle wouldn't become an issue. Of course we uncovered Mr. Peabody's easement in our title work, but quickly determined that this supposed encumbrance had no legal standing. First, no easement had ever been granted in writing and/or recorded as such. Second, in order for such an easement to exist, the Peabodys would have had to defend it continuously. Specifically, to quote the statute, it would be necessary that they maintain continuous, hostile and open possession in the face of opposition. No such defense has been mounted. Now Mr. VanMiddlesworth, eager to be neighborly and supportive of the natives' efforts to sustain themselves, has very generously

offered Mr. Peabody a pedestrian easement elsewhere on the property, in return of course for his relinquishing the dubious right he claims to the wharf. Inexplicably, Mr. Peabody has declined."

"Well as it happens," continued Muffin, "my old man was aware of the need to lay claim to the right of way and about the need to be hostile about it. Being in the habit of settin' on the porch after dinner and having a smoke and a glass of beer, he drove or walked down to the wharf damn near every evenin' dependin' on the weather, and pissed overboard in full view of the Ingerson house, figurin' that was a pretty clear way to demonstrate the needed hostility. For a while old man Ingerson hollered at Paw about what an annoyance that was, but then he just give up and turned his chair in a different direction. Since Paw died, 15 years now, I've done the same thing. And another thing, Mr. Midworthyness here did offer me an alternative way to get to the shore. Here it is in writin'. First of all, unlike the wharf I'm usin' now, the path he wants me to use is over in the nor'west corner where there's no deep water 'cept at full tide. Second, it describes a pedestrian easement three feet wide so the only way I can get a trap to the shore or back is to park up on the road and lug one to a time over my head lengthwise. I fish 600 traps. Finally, the easement expires when I do, leavin' my boys with no place to fish from."

Louie spoke up. "Madame Chair, I move the question." While a second was being called for, Louie reluctantly retrieved the Uncle Henry's and his bandanna from his new coat and offered it back to Opee. "You'll be wantin' your jacket back," he said.

---

*A regular contributor to* Working Waterfront, **Phil Crossman** *lives and writes on Vinalhaven.*

*Mouth of Strawberry Creek, from Stowe's sketchbook of 1859-87.*

# *Writer as Painter*

From the shore of Casco Bay 150 years ago, Harriet Beecher Stowe
painted a scene that is still recognizable today

RANDY PURINTON

*"Casco Bay," probably painted from the earlier sketch.*

Harriet Beecher Stowe learned painting when she was 16 because she thought she might teach the subject at her sister Catherine's school in Hartford, Connecticut. Instead, she taught English and later she became famous as the author of the anti-slavery novel Uncle Tom's Cabin, written while she and her family were living in Brunswick, Maine, a little more than 150 years ago.

Painting became a lifelong hobby, but only one of her works recalls her time in Maine—an oil painting titled "Casco Bay." It hangs above a bay window in her bedroom in the Stowe House in Hartford.

The seascape in the painting is very similar to the view looking south from the mouth of Strawberry Creek, on the road between North Harpswell and Orr's Island. Stowe would have traveled this road between Brunswick and Orr's Island, the setting for her only Maine-based novel, *The Pearl of Orr's Island.* Stowe passed that way at least once, drawing a pencil sketch of a tree beside it, titled "Ghost Pine on the way to Orr's Island."

Stowe rendered two versions of the scene. One is in her sketchbook, which contains works from 1859-1887. This gray-tone work shares the same basic details of the painting: a little island in the center, points of land stretching toward the center of the Sound and a few sailing vessels drifting in calm water. There is the suggestion a lighthouse or tower on the horizon behind the island and to the left in the sketch, but it is merely a mysterious blot.

"Casco Bay" was probably painted after the gray-tone piece; artists frequently develop paintings from sketches. In the painting Stowe multiplies the number of sailing vessels, adds a curious sailor in the foreground and magnifies the blot on the horizon until it becomes a tower. The tower still stands on Little Mark Island, at the entrance to Merriconeag Sound, just south of Harpswell Sound, and easily distinguishes the island in the center of Stowe's painting from all others.

The tall, hollow stone pyramid, painted white, had been built as an aid to navigation by the U.S. Government in 1827, 22 years before the Stowes moved to Brunswick from Cincinnati. About seven miles distant from Strawberry Creek, the tower is described on a modern chart as a monument 74 feet tall. It is in line with a view that begins at Strawberry Creek, passes south over a little island and follows the centerline of Harpswell and Merriconeag Sounds. We know that Stowe passed near Little Mark Island because her description of nearby Eagle Island in *The Pearl Of Orr's Island* had to have been written by someone who visited the area. In her painting, Stowe brought the tower closer.

Though life for the Stowe family in Brunswick was hard, she recalled many years later in a letter that, "...two healthier and happier years I never had... and the Maine people I loved. I traveled a good deal with Mr. Stowe when he went preaching and in the wildest most retired parts [we] found books, a culture, and cultured people—a most interesting race they were—bright as quartz crystals..."

Harriet Beecher Stowe was not as prolific or even as skilled a painter as she was a writer. Still, she saw little difference between writing and painting. As she wrote the novel that would bring her fame she said, "My vocation is simply that of a painter, and my object will be to hold up in the most lifelike and graphic manner possible Slavery... There is no arguing with pictures, and everybody is impressed by them..."

*Randy Purinton is a frequent contibutor to* Island Journal *and* Working Waterfront.

# "TECH"
## goes to Chicago

### In 1893, a Casco Bay steamer traveled the Erie Canal to the Columbian Exposition

## DAVID D. PLATT

*B. R. T. Collins in his Naval Reserve uniform*

To a budding engineer contemplating his summer plans for 1893, no place on Earth beckoned more brightly than the World's Columbian Exposition in Chicago. Powered and lit by electricity, designed by architects Daniel Burnham and Louis Sullivan, showcasing the first Ferris wheel, the exposition signaled to the world that the young, modern United States and its burgeoning technology had arrived.

"Practically all instructors and students at MIT were making plans during the preceding winter to go to Chicago during the summer," reported a 26-year-old instructor at the Massachusetts Institute of Technology. "There were special trains, special hotels, excursions for a week at the Fair…"

Someone at MIT suggested that a group make the trip from Boston to Chicago by water, "going down the coast to New York, up the Hudson River and through the Erie Canal and Great Lakes to Chicago." The young instructor knew the vessel the friend had in mind. "The FIRE FLY would not be large enough to stand possible storms on the lakes," he asserted. Then he suggested the possibility of chartering a larger steamer that could navigate the lakes safely, but still be able "to go through the smallest lock on the Erie Canal."

The cruise of the CADET was born.

*A painting of the CADET sporting MIT colors, a "T" (for "Tech") on her stack and a special burgee on the bow commemorates the Maine steamer's memorable cruise to Chicago. Illustrations courtesy of Eldon C. Mayer*

*Collins at MIT, where he apparently played baseball*

Bertrand R.T. (Bert) Collins was born in York, Maine, in 1866. He was a member of MIT's class of 1888, and became an instructor in the school's Steam Engineering Laboratory shortly after he graduated. Fascinated by ships from an early age, he had spent summers on Casco Bay and passed his test to be a Licensed Pilot for Steam Vessels Under 10 Tons in Portland in 1891 while still teaching at MIT. The lure of a 3,000-mile trip to Chicago and back aboard a steamer was irresistible.

The CADET was an excursion vessel belonging to the Casco Bay Island Steamboat Co. of Portland—predecessor of today's Casco Bay Lines. She had been built as a private steam yacht for service on the Hudson River in the West Point, N.Y., area (hence her name), but by 1893 had joined the five-ship Casco Bay fleet. "She is a boat of fine appearance, perfectly seaworthy and capable of developing high speed when necessary," Collins told MIT students in a written description of his proposed "expedition."

Initially Collins envisioned something more sedate than an excursion boat full of young students. "A meeting of instructors only" was called, "to see if enough of them would be interested to fill a steamer of proper size with them exclusively." Twelve faculty members showed up and decided to form an organization they called the "Technology Steamer Excursion to the World's Fair."

The group elected Collins treasurer and manager. In a single sentence indicative of an organized engineering mind, he was then instructed "to obtain all necessary information regarding steamboats available and cost of chartering for the trip to Chicago and return with ten days to two weeks' stay in Chicago, as well as all additional costs such as captain and crew, coal, water, steward's and cook's outfits, berths, cots, bedding, food, pilots on canal and lakes, permit for navigating canal, anchorage at Chicago, flags, printing, etc., in order to make a close estimate of the total cost and cost per passenger for all expenses except admission to the Fair on which we hoped to obtain some concession on account of the educational character of the trip."

And so Bert Collins went to work, corresponding with steamship companies in New York, Philadelphia and Baltimore as well as Portland before settling on the CADET at a charter rate of $36 per day including captain, crew of six, coal and water, "with the boat fitted up to take care of 35 people, 22 passengers and 13 in the crew—the remaining six of the crew not furnished by the Steamboat Co., would be a cook, steward and four waiters."

As winter progressed, however, the faculty members who had signed up began to change their minds. "One after another began to give reasons why they could not go," Collins recalled in his later account of the trip. " 'Going with his fiancé's family,' 'going with a camping outfit,' 'going with Raymond & Whitcomb [a tour company],' 'going to a special Fair hotel,' etc., etc. So I was turned down by all the instructors. I think the real reason was that they had no confidence in my ability to make a correct estimate and carry the plan through to success. This thought made me mad and I decided to go through the scheme, leaving all the instructors out and taking students only."

On April 10, Collins placed a copy of a printed "circular" in the mailboxes of all MIT students. "Your careful attention is invited," he wrote, "to the following statement of the arrangements which have been made in relation to the plan for a party representing the Massachusetts Institute of Technology to make an excursion to the World's Columbian Exposition by steamer during the month of June."

Collins then proceeded to describe the CADET (she would be "fitted up in as fine a manner as possible for this special occasion"), the route (the Erie Canal and the Great Lakes) and the accommodations ("four cabins, one to be used by the crew and steward, another as a dining saloon, the other two...fitted with berths, are well ventilated and have toilet rooms connected"). The CADET had to be back in Maine by the end of June, so the students would travel by train from Boston to Buffalo, N.Y., to save time. Eastbound, they could travel all the way to Boston aboard the CADET.

"Everything furnished by the Steward's department will be strictly first class and the best the market affords," Collins told prospective members of his tour. "Any desiring to take bicycles with them for use at Chicago and along the Erie Canal can do so for there will be sufficient storage room for all such. The chances for using a camera on such a trip will be innumerable, both on the Hudson, Canal and Lakes, as well as at Chicago. Any and all musical instruments played by any of the party will also be very welcome to enliven the evenings on the lake front..."

Collins's salesmanship worked. "The day following the issue of this circular," he reported later, "students began to come into my office and hand me $20 each for their initial payment. Two weeks before the date of our departure from Boston, I had all the money in the bank from the 23 passengers to pay for the trip."

In addition, there were sufficient funds to buy a 12-gauge bronze cannon, the idea being to fire salutes from the deck of the CADET at appropriate times.

MIT administered its last examinations for the spring term on May 31, and at 6:30 that evening the 23 students who had signed up for the Chicago "expedition" met at the train station in Fitchburg, outside of Boston. They tagged and checked their trunks and bicycles, received sleeping car berth tickets and boarded the "Scotland," a special car attached to a train that left (on time) at 7 p.m.

*Summer horseplay, Casco Bay, circa 1891.*

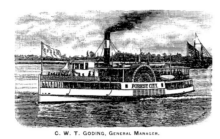

*During the winter before the cruise, Collins carried on a lengthy correspondence with officials of the Casco Bay Steamboat Company concerning the terms of the charter and details, such as whether the* CADET *would fit through the locks of the Erie Canal.*

If they fired their cannon from the train there's no record of it. But as they passed through the communities of eastern and central Massachusetts, the students made absolutely certain the locals knew who they were and where they were going. "At Fitchburg, Athol, Gardiner and other cities and towns where we made stops," Collins wrote, "nearly all stepped off on the platform and gave the various Tech yells, the general order being the 'M.I.T.' yell ending with 'Technology,' then the short yell with 'Chicago,' then the short yell again with the name of the city or town where we were..."

In Rotterdam Junction, New York, the "Scotland" was switched to another train, and by 6 o'clock the next morning (June 1), "all were up and watching with interest the Erie Canal and the surrounding country a little east of Syracuse, where we arrived at 7:10 a.m. just on time. A grand rush was made for the restaurant which was quickly cleared of a large stock of edibles..."

Shortly after noon the party reached Buffalo, where they were met by the steward and pilot who would accompany them aboard the CADET. The vessel had left Portland two weeks earlier.

The students, the pilot and the steward walked down Main St. to the wharf where the CADET lay, spruced-up as promised by Bert Collins. "The CADET presented a fine appearance as she lay at the wharf," he wrote in his account of the trip. "At the bow was the Union Jack and a white flag with 'Cadet' in large red letters. At the stern was the Stars and Stripes and a flag with CBSB Co. in red letters. The 'T' in cardinal red on the silver gray band around the stack looked fine, and a general 'yachtish' look prevailed both on deck and in the cabins."

He may or may not have told his passengers about it in advance, but Collins's correspondence with Casco Bay Steamboat Co.'s general manager reveals that he took pains to specify how that "silver gray band around the stack" should look. The red "T," of course, stood for "Tech," MIT's nickname at the time. Under the terms of its contract, the company was obliged to repaint the stack for the trip.

The cannon, which had arrived aboard the train, was hastily transported down to the ship where it "welcomed us upon our arrival, being manned by Mr. B. L. Keith," a member of the party. Once aboard, the group sat down for dinner—vegetable soup, roast ribs of beef, potatoes, turnips, radishes, bread and butter pudding, tea and coffee, strawberries and cream—scrutinized by a few good citizens of Buffalo.

"A crowd of 100 or more gathered on the wharf and with a good deal of curiosity watched us during our dinner as all the windows of the main saloon were open on account of the heat," Collins writes. "With booming of cannon, fluttering of flags and Technology cheers we steamed out of the dock and were soon on the broad expanse of Lake Erie..."

Lake Erie, relatively shallow, is known for its large waves and the fine dinner, alas, may not have been the right thing for a party not accustomed to such conditions. By the next morning (June 2), "all but 4 or 5 of those on board, 35 in all, were more or less seasick; consequently considerable food was saved for later hunger but some already eaten was turned over to the fish..."

Other adventures followed: the Detroit River; a visit to Detroit, where the engineering students admired two huge electrical towers; crossing Lake St. Clair; two groundings in fog in the St. Clair River that caused a nine-hour delay and cost the pilot $27 from his wages. By June 4 they were in Lake Huron, followed by "the Straights of Mackinaw," Milwaukee, Racine, Evanston and, finally, the pier at the Exposition in Chicago on June 6 at 7:45 p.m.

"We immediately landed and entered the Exposition grounds which were illuminated for the first time that evening. We went into the Electrical Building," Collins reports. "Heard Sousa's Band."

The CADET remained tied up at the pier for ten days, allowing the MIT students and the crew to enjoy the Exposition without ferrying back and forth to the steamer as they had expected. They ate meals aboard and "passed out and in again" through the Exposition gate at will, paying the 50-cent admission fee only once each day. All of this was contrary to the regulations, according to Collins, and "was due to the statements I made to the

Casco Bay Steamboat Company.

Passenger Line Carrying the U. S. Mail

—BETWEEN—

PORTLAND, MAINE, AND ISLANDS IN CASCO BAY.

C. W. T. GODING, General Manager.

GENERAL MANAGER'S OFFICE,

Portland, Me., March 7 1893

W A T Collins,
Mass Institute of Technology
Boston Mass

Dear Sir

Your letter of yesterday to hand have talked with our Directors and they have made up there minds that the Boat will be gone well into July and as that is all the time that we want her think we can not make a price unless we can have her in Portland July first if you can start or as to be back as soon as that I will make a price if not we shall have to be counted out as we must have here July and Aug

Yours truly
C W T Goding

*The company's busy summer schedule nearly scotched the negotiations, but the MIT group was able to guarantee the steamer's timely return.*

various officials in regard to the educational character of our expedition made up of students of science and engineering traveling in a body 3000 miles from the Atlantic coast to the metropolis of the mid-west and return."

Detailed as it is, Bert Collins's description of the trip doesn't account for his own whereabouts during the two weeks it took the CADET to reach Buffalo from Portland. He writes at one point as if he were riding the train with the other students, but elsewhere he describes what sounds like a westbound trip through the Erie Canal, which the train riders would have missed due to MIT's final exam schedule. In any event, he was aboard for the eastbound return trip through the canal.

"There was no unnecessary delay in passing through the canal," Collins explains, "due principally to the fact that Capt. McIntire [the pilot] had spent his entire life of 55 years on the canal after having been born on a canal boat, as it was the custom in the early days of canal-boat-ing for the families of the boat-men to make their homes in the cabins on the canal boats."

The official speed limit in the Erie Canal in 1893 was four miles per hour. Having an experienced pilot aboard seems to have allowed the CADET to move at six miles per hour, and—legally or otherwise—"we were able to travel at a speed of ten miles per hour between the hours of 10 p.m. and 6 a.m. in certain sections." Visibility might have been less, but so was the traffic.

Such high speed "caused a veritable 'tidal wave' to follow the ship," Collins reports. "This did no harm however to the farm lands through which we passed." Ever the engineer, he then explains why the wake was so large: the Erie Canal's standard width was 70 feet with a minimum depth of seven feet. CADET's draft was seven feet as well, and she "bumped along the bottom of the canal several times during our passage through it." The 96-foot CADET may, in fact, have been the largest vessel to pass through the canal

up to that time, and could be expected to displace a substantial amount of its limited water.

On Saturday, June 17, after 11 days at the Exposition, the CADET cast off her lines and set out again for Boston and Maine. "After a brilliant display of fireworks on the evening of Massachusetts Day," wrote A. D. Fuller, a reporter for the MIT student newspaper, *The Tech*, "and after a rattling Tech cheer the wonderful 'White City' [the Exposition] faded into the darkness. The excellent weather, the sights of various ports, the domino, checker, shooting and other tournaments, combined with gay spirits to shorten the lake trip, but all were glad to leave the boat at Lockport, N.Y., for a day at Niagara Falls."

Re-boarding at Rochester, the party proceeded along the Erie Canal to Syracuse, Utica, Albany, New York City, Newport and Martha's Vineyard, reaching Boston on June 29. "Considerable credit is due to Mr. B.R.T. Collins for originating and managing the party," wrote the student reporter. "With no experience in such matters, few would have had the courage and perseverance to carry out the plan."

Collins includes the *Tech* article, but no others, in his own typed, unpublished account now owned by his grandson, Eldon C. Mayer of Chebeague Island. "At this point I had planned to insert several clippings from the local papers in the cities where we stopped," he concludes, "but they have been misplaced. It is, perhaps, just as well for otherwise some might accuse me of blowing my horn too much."

Collins returned to MIT only briefly after the trip, resigning to accept an engineering position with Commonwealth Edison in Chicago.

The CADET returned to Casco Bay where she resumed her work as an excursion steamer. She was part of the Casco Bay Steamboat Co.'s fleet until 1903.

The cannon, after firing some 55 salutes, passed into Collins's possession as a way of evening up the accounts. After all bills had been paid, "it appeared that I had paid out approximately $17.50 more than I had received and as the cannon cost that amount I simply transferred [it] to my own personal property thus making an exact balance—in other words, the estimate I made of the total cost of the trip which my fellow instructors seemed to doubt the correctness of, proved to be correct 100 percent and the best estimate of my subsequent engineering career of nearly half a century."

*David D. Platt is editor of Island Journal.*

Of course, sometimes they do blow things up (though as a rule the property owners are compensated). Crowds turned out in Eastport to watch the "Murder in Small Town X" crew explode a fishing boat at one point, and drive a car off a pier at another. And although Michael Radcliffe's real property wasn't destroyed, he had the "kind of surreal" experience of watching a quarter-scale replica of Thurston's Wharf demolished by pounding water in a wave pool in Arizona (the trip was paid for by the "Storm of the Century" production company as part of his compensation for letting them shoot at his place). The operation cost millions of dollars, Radcliffe says, and took weeks of work—all for a few minutes of film time.

Hollywood is famous for going to great lengths to achieve the smallest details of the image it desires. The stories are mind-boggling.

David Greenberg, a teacher and filmmaker who lives in Rockland, uses this example in his classes: "Say you're filming a movie in Maine that takes place in the summer, but it's August when you're shooting and the leaves are starting to turn. Do you just work around it, do you change the story, or do you spray-paint the leaves? In 'Pet Sematary' (filmed in the Ellsworth area in 1988), they spray-painted all the leaves."

The radical difference in scale is one of the most unsettling things about Hollywood productions coming to small communities, partly because it's almost impossible for normal people to relate to the amounts of money thrown around. At the same time, when such a flurry of activity comes to town, when so much time and money are spent there, it can set everyone up for anti-climax.

While Rockland City Attorney Greg Dorr thought the city was represented "beautifully" in "In the Bedroom," he admits to letting himself feel a little jilted when the excitement of the production died down. "When they were gone, they were gone," he says. "I think I personally thought that this might be the start of a long-term relationship. Maybe Good Machine (the production company for "In the Bedroom") will buy the Strand Cinema. You have all these wonderful fantasies, that they will become some sort of ongoing presence in the community somehow. But when they were gone, they were gone. It's disconcerting to have such a major event come in and then one day just be gone."

*Ready to roll, Vinalhaven, 1947.*

The scale of even low-budget film productions is so foreign to most people, that when a crew lavishes what feels like a great deal of attention on your town, it's easy to feel you're the star of the show. When you eagerly view the final product and realize your community is just background—perhaps even unrecognizable—it can be deflating.

"You have to understand that you can watch them shoot Main Street Rockland all day, but eight hours of filming can add up to only two minutes of film," Arey points out. "That's up to the editor and the director...what we're seeing with our naked eye and what they're seeing through the lens are totally different. And I think that's why people are confused or let themselves get disappointed."

The experience of being filmed, of posing for the camera, and ultimately the experience of seeing yourself through the eyes of another, does not have to be negative. In fact, a community's sense of self, like a person's, is strongest when it's a combination of the way it sees itself and the way others see it. After all, others can see things in you that you forgot were there.

Which brings us back to Eastport. Despite the many differences between the city and the fictional town of Sunrise that appeared in the final product, and despite the hassles of accommodating an often demanding cast and crew, some say the process of getting gussied up, and the energy that saturated the community during the production, stirred something in the town.

"I guess family members of people who lived there came back because they heard this was going on," says Kathryn Smith, a member of the "Murder in Small Town X" crew. "It was just so neat for everybody to have the place lit up. I remember talking to some older people about the times when Eastport was like that. A lot of people said 'you know, we haven't seen it all lit up like this in years.' "

And so it happens that a statue that isn't real, and which basically has nothing to do with the town or its history, can serve as a reminder of better days.

"It's too bad they didn't leave their entire set of props here," says Eastport Town Manager Bud Finch, who fully expects the town to host more productions in the future. "They made the town look really nice—it was probably the most refreshing, hopeful look downtown has had in years. It was really that image that was left from the movie that's spurring people to try and revitalize downtown now. That was probably the key motivator, that people saw what it used to be like, because of the production."

Not everybody in Eastport likes the statue, and its future on Main Street is uncertain. But its persistence to this point does seem to have something to do with that resurgent pride that came with the bright lights and fresh paint. And, after all, why shouldn't it stay there? The truth is that the statue is as real as anything else: it is, in fact, an authentic movie prop.

*Nathan Michaud is Program Officer for Community Planning at the Island Institute.*

# The Little Fish That Couldn't

NAOMI SCHALIT

They are small fish, but they've caused big trouble over the last few years in Maine. The St. Croix River's alewives have been the focus of a bitter battle stretching from the lakes and streams of the Downeast region all the way to the corridors of power in Ottawa and Washington. Downeast fishing guides argued—despite scientific evidence to the contrary—that native alewives in the upper St. Croix watershed threatened to out-compete or devour the smallmouth bass, an introduced species whose presence provided fishing guides with a good living. So the fishing guides convinced the legislature to block spawning alewives from the river's upper reaches.

At its simplest, the conflict was about whether to allow migrating alewives access to their ancestral spawning grounds. But underlying the fight were larger questions: Is it right to favor an introduced species over a native one, simply because humans can make money off of the introduced species? Is the economic worth of a species its only measure of value?

Tim Andrews is an environmental engineer at the Domtar mill in Woodland. He's worked there for 26 years, since it belonged to the Georgia-Pacific Company. Wearing a helmet and protective glasses, he strides through the bowels of this rambling and musty brick complex whose huge, water-powered turbines have been turning since the 1920s to provide the power for making pulp and paper.

Andrews emerges from the dark and steamy mill into the outdoors. The noise of rushing water is deafening. He's standing next to a fish ladder, built in the 1960s to help migrating fish make their way upstream. Without it, the fish couldn't pass over the dam. And at the mouth of the fishway, where salmon and alewives would normally enter, Andrews points to a couple of flat wooden boards placed smack in the path of the fish.

"You can see the water rushing over that gate," he says. "That's too high, so the alewives can't make it up over it."

The alewife, or *alosa pseudoharengus*, is a river herring. Silvery and sleek, alewives migrate from saltwater to fresh during their spawning runs, which in Maine generally range from April through late June. They lay their eggs above the head of tide in the lakes, streams and ponds that constitute the upper watershed of an estuary. And historically, their runs were an astonishing sight all along the rivers of the Eastern Seaboard, from the mid-Atlantic states to Nova Scotia. The St. Croix was no exception.

"In the early eighties, you'd come out and see the water just boiling," he says. "The water'd be black with 'em and then after they spawned, coming down through the water wheels would be millions of little tiny alewives. There'd be gulls here, there'd be fish, some sort of ducks—everything would be feeding on the little alewives. It was a regular feeding ground."

Alewives are food for eagles, osprey and cormorants; they are prey for any number of small mammals that haunt the banks of Maine's rivers as well. And, scientists say, they provide much-needed cover for salmon smolts when the juvenile salmon migrate out of the state's rivers to the ocean. They're what some biologists call a "cornerstone species," providing the resource base to support much of a river's ecosystem.

But that's not how the fishing guides of Washington County and their allies see alewives.

During the warmer months, those guides gather every morning at the Pine Tree Store in Grand Lake Stream, a tiny town tucked into the dark green woods of eastern Maine. They show up to buy flies and insect repellant, soft drinks and whatever else they might need for a day of guiding visiting fishermen on the water.

This is angling country, world-renowned. Fishermen from across the globe come to cast their lines into the region's numerous lakes. Dave Irving has been guiding here since 1971.

"There's so much diversity," he says. "You can fish lake trout. You can fish brook trout, landlocked salmon. Oh, you can fish at a different lake every day of the month, and if you had thirty days to fish, you could go to a different place every day."

And in the world of Grand Lake Stream fishing guides, there's one fish revered above all others: the bass. Introduced to this lake system in the 19th century, bass are the cornerstone species of this region's economy, according to guide Louie Cataldo.

"This whole area depends on the bass," he says. "We built our businesses around the bass."

The Downeast region—and Washington county in particular—is not what you would call economically well-off. In fact, it's one of the most depressed regions in the United States. So the bass are more than just an incidental part of the economy in this corner of the state. As one local guide put it, the fishing industry up here is "a one-horse economy riding on the back of a limping horse." And more than 15 years ago, disaster struck. The lucrative bass fishery in Spednic Lake, further up

*Photographs by Bill Curtsinger (2)*

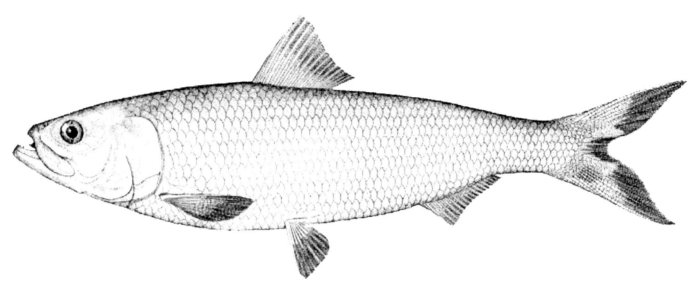

*The alewife, or* alosa pseudoharengus, *is a river herring.*

the watershed, crashed. The fish simply disappeared. And the fishing guides blamed alewives who, they said, either ate the bass or out-competed them. The alewives, whose numbers had plummeted over the past century because of damming and pollution in the St. Croix, were in the process of being restored to the river's upper reaches when the Spednic Lake crash happened. And despite scientific evidence from across the state that alewives and bass live happily together in other watersheds, a rural legend was born: the alewives killed the bass. State Rep. Albion Goodwin put it succinctly:

"We have piranhas in South America; we also have piranhas in North America, and they're called alewives. They are eating machines, they eat everything in the body of water."

The Grand Lake guides were convinced that alewives posed a threat to their livelihoods. From their point of view, alewives were a virtually useless part of the St. Croix's ecosystem. Guide Bill Gillespie:

"The bass is a sport fish where people can make a living fishing for them. Whereas alewife is, in most part, a junk fish. It's more of a forage fish that comes up here just to breed and go back to the ocean, and eat everything in between."

So in 1995, the fishing guides took their case to the state legislature: choose alewives or bass, they said, and the guides knew which fish they wanted. A bill was presented to stop funding for St. Croix alewife restoration efforts, which by then had brought alewife numbers in the river back up to the millions. And in what many now say was a midnight, back channel effort with no public input, that bill was changed at the last minute to instruct fisheries managers to block alewives altogether from the upper river. Rep. Royce Perkins of Penobscot was a member of the

Inland Fisheries and Wildlife Committee, which considered and passed the bill:

"The original bill that came to us didn't say anything about blocking the fish," he says. "As it turned out, what we passed was definitely a blockage, and that does concern me."

The blockage concerned more than just an isolated member of the Maine Legislature. By 2001, evidence had mounted that the alewife barriers at fishways on two dams had caused a serious decline in the fish's population. That got the interest of the federal government, which had—way back in the 1960s—helped pay for the fishways in the first place, in the interest of restoring native migratory fish to the St. Croix. And it also got the interest of the Canadian government, because the St. Croix river is the international boundary between Canada and the United States in the Downeast region. Arguably Maine's actions were hurting alewives that belonged to Canada as well. Ron Essig is with the U.S. Fish and Wildlife Service's federal aid division:

"The purpose of those facilities was to provide upstream passage of salmon, alewives and shad," he said in early 2001, "and the law that was passed by the state of Maine back in 1995 seems to be putting the use of those fishways against the intended purpose."

Pressure mounted both from the federal government and the Canadians to do something about the situation. A cross-border group of fisheries officials—including representatives from Maine's Department of Inland Fisheries and Wildlife, as well as the Marine Resources Department—hashed out a plan to restore a limited number of alewives up above the blockages, and participants in that process hoped that that plan would be the basis for legislation to unblock the fishways.

But when a bill to adopt that plan was introduced in the Maine Legislature, all hell broke loose.

Hearings on the bill were packed, mostly with people who wanted to keep the alewives out of the upper river. The Canadians showed up to testify as well, and in an uncharacteristically confrontational move, one of their officials—Larry Marshall, from the Canadian federal Department of Fisheries and Oceans—told the legislators that if they didn't vote to pass alewives above the Woodland Dam, the Canadians would truck them around. State Department officials in Washington, D.C. were following the issue, as were their counterparts in Ottawa.

Few things can rile up the Maine Legislature like fish, deer or moose. In this case, the equation went as follows: If the legislature voted to restore alewives, it was voting to steal the one economic lifeline left to Washington County. If it did that, said one guide, then "we might as well pack up and go home." Pat Keliher, who heads the sportfishermen's group called the Coastal Conservation Association, says "this was probably the longest floor debate in the house...the energy was extremely high, it was based on, in many cases, incorrect facts."

The ante was upped even further when the federal government announced it would withhold millions of dollars in federal aid if the blockages weren't removed, since the fishways it had helped fund obviously weren't being used for their intended purpose. But if the Feds intended that argument to help push the legislation along, it didn't. It just got legislators' backs up, and some grew even more determined to resist alewife restoration.

In the end, the legislation failed. Washington County representative George

*Continued on page 94*

# SICKLE BIRD

*The peregrine falcon's eye sees all,
reveals nothing*

*Story by*
SUSAN HAND SHETTERLY

*Illustrations by*
REBECCA GOODALE

At six in the morning, mid-October, before the change to standard time, it is dark and cold in the village on Monhegan Island. The stars shine. The night wind has dropped and the beat of the surf and the drone of the village generator replace the sounds of thrashing trees. A person awake in one of the quiet houses might notice, if she stepped outside at this hour, the merest infusion of light into the darkness, what sailors refer to as nautical twilight. She might think of the island cliffs to the east, where the sun will first show itself.

Night-migrants, small birds beating their way south in scattered flocks, have already located the darker outline of rock against the dark water and sky. They are heading toward it, setting down, folding themselves into the raspberry and blackberry tangles of the headlands. She might think of a peregrine falcon perched on a spruce snag on a jut of rock above the waves, its blunt form like a chunk of stone. She might imagine the dark eyes of the bird opening, its head tilting to follow the shadowy form of a songbird flying in. One, another, and one more. It is not light enough for the falcon to fly, although, as a dawn and dusk hunter, the bird will bolt from its perch before long. Right now, it stretches a broad, finely tapered wing, turns its head back into the feathers of its shoulder and its eyes close. She first saw peregrines in the late afternoon out on the headlands, two birds playing high over the cliffs at Black Head. She sat on a rock close to the water at Squeaker Cove and watched them as the wind came in from the east and rode up the verticals to create the warm currents through which they dove and circled, teased a gull foolish enough to join them and, in a blazingly fast stoop, one after another, dropped away to the other side of the island.

When I think of peregrine falcons and their relationship with men, I don't think of Sumaria in 750 B.C. and the ancient falconers flying their birds over dry scrub. I think of the British and French falconers who served in World War II. They flew their birds against German carrier pigeons. I try to get my mind around the idea of a falconer in the trenches, setting the bird he's trained for years onto his fist, unhooding it, letting the big eyes adjust, feeling the bird lift off into the unsafe air, its jesses flapping at its feet.

Falcons are the wildest birds we can imagine. For centuries humans applauded that wildness and appropriated what they could of it through falconry. But with the growth of game reserves and small farms, birds of prey became adversaries. Shooting "hawks" was rural civic duty in this country and in Europe well into the early 20th century. In the 18th and 19th centuries, in America, pressure was put on nesting birds by egg and specimen collectors whose energetic passion to explore every part of the New World was matched by an easy joy of killing and collecting its creatures. Falcons just couldn't get away from us.

But falconry and gunnery and bird collections didn't hurt them the way organo-hydrocarbons did. And we didn't even know then that our pesticides—one of the heralded discoveries of the war

*Peregrines are top-of-the-food-chain predators.*

years—were poisoning the food chain, destroying some birds outright, and thinning the eggs of others. This was the most effective assault, more deadly than anything that had proceeded it, a silent and, at first, mysterious killer. When the time came, in the 1970s, to save the peregrines of Europe and the United States by captive breeding and the release procedure called "hacking," it was the falconers on both sides of the Atlantic—people who knew the birds intimately—who developed many of the techniques for reintroduction. One might call it another war effort. But this was a brand new kind of war.

Peregrines are top-of-the-food-chain predators. Flying cheetahs. Orcas of the air. The food triangle on which they perch starts with fields that ripen into seeds and grains, and provide habitat and food for insects; and with rivers and lakes and bays that grow algae, insects, mollusks and fish. Birds eat the grains and the seeds and the insects from the fields. Ducks and grebes, geese and wading birds feed in and along the water. Falcons eat these birds. Whatever nutrition they receive is concentrated. Whatever poisons sprayed on the fields or drained into the waterways are concentrated, too, and stored in the falcons' fat.

Even before the poisoning, peregrine falcons were rare. Ora Willis Knight, in his 1908 study of Maine birds, wrote that they probably nested only in Oxford, Penobscot, Washington and Hancock counties. One might have discovered a pair raising young in a scrape in the gravel on a remote cliff—they often inhabit the wildest, least humanly accessible places—or might have seen them in small numbers in fall migration, perhaps out on islands such as Monhegan where they follow the southward flow of birds, their primary food. Knight wrote of peregrines: "They are brave, audacious and dashing, flying 'like a bullet' after their prey." As with many others of his time, he was uneasy about birds of prey that might compete with the interests of men. He ends his monograph stating that peregrines eat ducks and chickens and grouse. Not a diet that would endear them to the hunter or the farmer.

In truth, the peregrine diet is more interesting and more varied. Pigeons are a favored food. So are northern flickers. When we were lucky enough to have the enormous flocks of passenger pigeons that reportedly darkened the skies, we had the perfect falcons to hunt them. Today feral pigeons of the cities have filled that gap for some of these birds.

Peregrines are sexually dimorphic, which means that one sex is bigger than the other. In this case, the larger bird is female. Ornithologists, puzzling over why this adaptation might work well for them, suggest that the smaller male is the more nimble flyer, and catches mostly songbirds, snatching them out of the air. This is good for a female brooding her young, and in need of a constant food supply for the chicks. The male brings her kinglets, swallows, thrushes, jays and sparrows, grabbing them in flight and carrying them to the aerie. When a female hunts, she can take on prey as large as a duck or a small goose. Size difference allows the falcon pair to hunt a large prey base.

Peregrines have nested on every continent except the Antarctic, adapting to habitat so flawlessly that within the species there are many subspecies, birds matched to the land where they breed. What a peregrine requires is open space, whether it is a vast bog in Finland, an abandoned castle on the tablelands of La Mancha, a butte in Idaho, a skyscraper in Chicago or Manhattan, or a rugged cliff with a narrow ledge on which the chicks fledge in Labrador or in Maine. And it needs a good, constant food supply.

*Anatum*, the subspecies honed through thousands of years to the northeastern landscape, has been lost to poisoning. Although these particular birds are still found in small numbers in the American West and in western Canada, the primary subspecies along the northwest coast is *pealei*. All nesting pairs of *anatum* from the Atlantic Ocean to the Mississippi River disappeared by the 1960s, due to pesticide poisoning. The peregrines playing above Monhegan and patrolling its headlands today breed in the high Arctic and migrate through. They are called *tundrius*. Or, if we're extraordinarily lucky, we may catch a glimpse of a new kind of peregrine: a banded bird of mixed parentage. It is the result of years and years of hard, slow work by biologists, environmentalists and falconers. The parents and grandparents of these birds began their lives in laboratories and in captive breeding programs. They were introduced into the homesites left vacant by *anatum*.

Charlie Todd, biologist at Maine Inland Fisheries and Wildlife, and overseer of the state peregrine reintroduction project, calls the birds that nest here "Heinz 57 peregrines," the offspring of a variety of subspecies, including some from Spain, from the northwest coast of the United States, from New Zealand and from Britain. From 1984 through 1997, 153 young were released into the state. Today we have 15 nesting pairs, the first and second generations of the reintroduced birds. It is a healthy number, reinforced by spillover back and forth between Maine and the reintroduced populations in Vermont and New Hampshire. Todd mentions that we have lost some birds to Boston and New York City, where they nest on skyscrapers and feed on feral pigeons. There are no records of peregrines nesting on Monhegan.

The paths direct people to the height of land. No peregrine pair would tolerate people looking down onto its chicks, although with the heavy use of the island in migration by the birds, there is always the possibility that a pair, in early April, might choose a ledge on the headlands on which to lay their eggs. Buildings in big cities are another question. Visual buffers and one-way glass have been set up to keep nesting falcons from being overwhelmed by human presence. But the pleasures of having a nesting pair outside a skyscraper window may begin to pall in early summer as more and more pigeons are torn to bits and fed delicately to the young. And the problem of poisoning continues. We have dioxin in our rivers from the paper mills. We have migrating birds coming up the eastern flyway from Central and South America where the pesticides that defeated *anatum* are still sold and liberally used. The migrating falcons and the birds they eat bring the poisons back home to us, stored in their bodies.

"Falcon" is from the Latin, "*falcatus*," meaning "sickle," and refers to the feet. Anyone who has seen a falcon up close, or has had the privilege of holding one on the fist, has noted the big, curved talons and the big, curved toes. But falcons are not clumsy-footed. They use the feet to kill, or to grasp struggling prey as they lean down to slice their notched bills into the spinal column to sever it. Some peregrines have a habit of making loose fists and punching small birds out of the air, then plunging beneath the falling bird and snatching it before it hits the ground. The peregrine wing shape is sickle-like as well: thick where it attaches to the body, acutely tapered, with especially long primary feathers. The adjustments the birds make to the wing—as top-speed, gorgeously acrobatic fliers—can temporarily alter that basic shape, but when a peregrine is playing over an island, plunging down toward the water headfirst, then curving away from it just in time, and rising again, it looks like an anchor tossed weightlessly into the sky.

———

I dress in the dark and slip out of my room, out of the inn, into the cold morning. I walk the trail along the western edge of the island, past unlit houses. It is a narrow trail close to the water and crosshatched with the roots of juniper. Small shadowy birds rise off it ahead of me. They make abrupt, sharp sounds, like sparrows. At Christmas Cove, I find the sun just breaking above the water's horizon, a blinding light. And on one of the ledges by the water, I pick up the remains of a blackburnian warbler, a blaze of feathers, orange and yellow and white, and a tiny, blood-soaked bill, and a thin, black leg.

I am sure it is a falcon kill. More feathers are scattered over the rock where the falcon ripped them free to get at the knob of meat. I shield my eyes and peer in the direction of the sun, and spot a falcon sitting on a high ledge a hundred yards ahead. It is just a thick black silhouette at first, until I move up into the trees behind it, and see it with the sun shining on it: a coal-black military hood, black moustaches, a gleaming white throat and a checkered black and white belly. The wings are blue-black. The feet are terribly yellow. It wears no band. It is *tundrius*, the bird from the Arctic north. The gorgeous bird is calm, unperturbed by me and by the clot of blackburnian feathers stuck to its hooked beak and ruffling in the wind.

Much has been written of the peregrine eye—big, black, its expression—well, expressionless. Maybe not expressionless. Maybe impassive. After all these birds have gone through by our hands, a free, wild peregrine can still look at a person across the vast space of our differences as if she were no more or less to it than a rock or a tree. The bird turns its head quickly and stares at me. There is no fear in it. No curiosity. The eye just notes that I am here, at a certain distance, and then the big bird looks away, out over the water to the long, thin raft of eiders. I am watching it watch eiders. We are very, very quiet in our watching for about ten minutes. And then, simply, it flies away. Lifts up, flaps its big stiff wings twice. Is gone. Beside me I hear the soft bell-like sounds of little birds. Yellow-rumped warblers, probably migrants from the night just passed, hop and flit at the edges where the old spruces meet the bare rock. They are hunting small flies that are just now starting to stir in the sunlight.

**Susan Hand Shetterly** *is author of* New Year's Owl *and other books.*

# Mines, Murals

# and Tourists

## In Newfoundland, an island town works to save itself from extinction

*Story and Photographs by*
NANCY GRIFFIN

Newfoundland's Bell Island easily lives up to its nickname, "Belle of the Bay," with its rocky cliffs, rolling fields and endless, ever-changing vistas of Conception Bay. However, the beauty and tranquility mask a serious problem on the island—there are too few jobs, and the lack of employment opportunities means young people have no future there.

The population has been draining away steadily for more than thirty years, ever since the drastic, sudden demise of the island's only industry. Looking at Bell Island now, with its population of 3,200 and the occasional closed-up buildings that crop up in the large spaces between well-tended homes, a first-time observer would never guess that the island was once one of Newfoundland's most prosperous communities. That it had a population of 24,000 and a thriving iron-mining industry, that it was not the cod moratorium that decimated the population.

*In "The Hub of the Island," artist John Littlejohn portrays the center of town in its heyday of the 1940s.*

Unlike most small communities in Newfoundland, Bell Island—six miles long, two miles wide and situated only three miles off the mainland across The Tickle—was not dependent on the 500-year-old cod fishery that collapsed in 1992. Bell Islanders quit fishing before the turn of the last century to labor in the mines for a steady, year-round wage, doing work that, if grueling, was more predictable than fishing.

Then, following decades of prosperity, the last mine closed quickly and unexpectedly in 1966. Experts say the rich supply of ore could have been mined for another hundred years, but the company's owners decided it was cheaper to produce iron elsewhere.

The population of the island plummeted as out-of-work miners and young people with no prospects boarded the ferry for the mainland, often heading for points far west—usually Ontario—from which most would never return. At the same time, the provincial government began an island resettlement program throughout Newfoundland, offering to pay island homeowners a pittance for their property and a small moving bonus. Given Bell Island's sudden hard times, many residents reluctantly accepted the government offer and the year-round population was further decimated.

"A huge population went to Ontario, especially Cambridge. Now a few of the people who left are retiring and moving home to live on Bell Island again," said Paul Connors, director of tourism and economic development for the island. "Seven new homes have been built in the past few years. That's a housing boom for Bell Island."

Bell Island's story is in many ways typical of small island communities everywhere: the way of life changes, jobs go,

people leave and the island becomes a bittersweet memory, a story for parents to hand down to their children.

But the old tale won't have the same sad ending on this island if the remaining residents have anything to say about it. A hardy group of people, who have so far managed to cling to their beloved island like barnacles to a rock, have hopes and plans to restore Bell Island to economic viability and cultural vibrancy.

The first part of the plan, already in progress, involves using art to attract visitors. Tourists may now walk, drive or take a bus tour to view murals that illustrate the island's rich mining history, tour a mineshaft and see the tools of the trade in a museum built over the shaft.

Despite the dominance of mining, residents are quick to point out that the island has more to offer. For instance, Bell Island is the only place on the North American continent that was attacked during World War II. In 1942, torpedoes from German U-boats sank four ships at the dock where 80,000 tons of iron awaited shipping. A stone Seamen's Memorial at Lance Cove bears witness to the 69 men who were killed.

Near the ferry landing, a natural walking trail leads visitors past guns installed during the war to protect later ore shipments, as well as a grotto that marks the former location of one of the oldest churches in North America. The island's town is Wabana, the name given to the island by its first residents, meaning "The Place Where the Sun First Shines."

Ball lightning, a rare meteorological phenomenon, struck Bell Island in 1978, leaving large craters that are still there today. Scientists and military personnel from as far away as Los Alamos, New Mexico, have visited the island to study the site.

Yousef Karsh, the world-renowned portrait photographer from Montreal, visited Bell Island during the 1950s and was so taken with the place, he photographed many miners and donated the portraits to the town. A large collection of original Karsh portraits now graces the walls of the mining museum.

## MURALS

Attracting tourists to an otherwise impoverished town through the use of murals is not original to Bell Island. Chemainus, British Columbia, a West Coast town with the same population, created a highly successful tourist industry with a mural project in the 1980s.

Brian Brook, a Bell Island resident, traveled to Chemainus, saw the murals and the potential, and brought the idea home, figuring his community's story was equally compelling.

In 1983, Chemainus lost its only industry—a sawmill that had employed most of the residents for 120 years. Townspeople quickly launched the Festival of Murals, attracted public and private investors, and covered the sides of many town buildings with large paintings depicting the lumbering history. The murals now attract more than 350,000 visitors each year.

Besides population figures and historic dependence on a single industry, however, Bell Island and Chemainus do not have a lot in common. The mill in Chemainus was modernized and re-opened two years after it closed, restoring many jobs and guaranteeing the town's economic survival. And Chemainus is not an island.

"Living on an island is a blessing in many ways, and problematic in others," said Ken Kavanagh, retired teacher and lifelong Bell Island resident. "We're a microcosm of Newfoundland. Being sur-

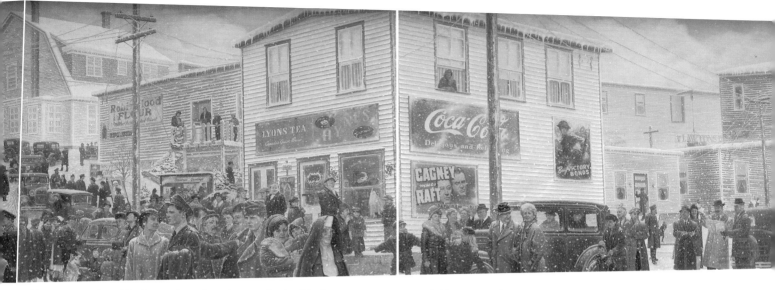

*The building adorned by the mural stands at the same site, but it's alone now—no stores, no shoppers, no movies.*

rounded by water creates an invisible barrier" that slows tourism and development.

When Bell Island residents began planning for the murals, they needed an accomplished, preferably well-known artist, to attract grant money and to give the project a healthy start.

"In 1990, I was on a 31-state tour of the U.S. with an exhibit of my wildlife paintings when I was asked if I would go Bell Island, my hometown, and train local artists to do murals," said John Littlejohn. "I had never painted a mural in my life."

Littlejohn left Bell Island at 13 years old, when he ran away from home to Toronto, determined to become an artist like his idol, Norman Rockwell. Self-taught, by 1990 he had become a successful wildlife artist and illustrator whose artistic adventures had taken him as far as the Arctic to paint polar bears.

"Brian Brook remembered seeing a brochure about my exhibit at my brother's house, so he contacted me," said Littlejohn, whose father worked for 40 years in the mines. "I arrived on Canada Day in 1991, figuring to stay a month or two. I left in February of 1999."

Upon arrival, expecting to paint his first and only mural—a giant portrait of miner Billy Parsons, affectionately known as "Uncle Billy"—Littlejohn found the wall had not been prepared properly and a mural painted on it would not have survived a year in Newfoundland's climate. Since redoing the wall would take the workers a month and a half, Littlejohn decided he might as well use the time to offer a few classes in materials and technique for the future painters. "But, I didn't tell my business manager!"

"When I heard about the project in 1990, I decided to go to Bell Island for a month to work with John," said artist Rick Murphy. "It really brought me back to my roots." Murphy's father was born on the island, moved away, but returned to buy a house and spend summers there. "I ended up dropping out of college and apprenticing with John. I stayed on the island for seven years."

The collaboration has become a business. In 1999, Murphy and Littlejohn became partners in D3 Artworks in Cambridge, Ontario, creating art for large corporate projects. Recent contracts involved Coca-Cola, Gordie Howe and the oldest ice hockey rink in North America.

The oldest Bell Island murals were painted directly on the walls of buildings, from which they are now peeling. Two replacements have been completed and are awaiting installation while islanders try to raise money to redo the rest, using longer-lasting materials and methods. The more recent island murals were painted on huge canvases, employing new techniques that include barriers for vapor and ultraviolet rays, and a clear, protective coating.

"Permanency and longevity are big things with John," said Murphy.

"The Hub of the Island," 80 feet long and eight feet high, was a "three-year labor of love" using the high-tech approach, said Littlejohn. "We built a lean-to around it and used heat and light to finish it. It was expensive, but worth it."

Unveiled in 1996, The Hub portrays the center of town in its heyday of the 1940s. Snow falls on well-dressed Christmas shoppers who crowd the sidewalks. The street is filled with new cars and lined by busy stores. A poster advertises the latest Cagney movie. The building adorned by the mural is located where this busy scene took place, but the building stands alone now with no stores and no shoppers and no movies.

So far, the murals reflect the island's mining history. "Uncle Billy," his smiling face topped by a miner's hat, has become the symbol for Bell Island. His contagious smile not only beams from the huge mural on the side of the town hall, but also from posters advertising the island's attractions.

"While we were doing the murals, the American visitors were so generous," said Littlejohn. "They would give from their hearts and donate $50 or $100—on the spot. They understood what we were trying to do."

Islanders are hoping to raise enough money to build a new museum where all the murals can be replicated indoors, for an interactive experience. They also hope to fund more murals that will tell the island's entire chronological history.

"It's coming full circle," said Murphy. "The planets will align, inevitably, and one day everything will click for them."

## MINING

Mining on Bell Island is not just a memory or a motif for murals, but a museum. Situated above the entrance to a mineshaft, a mining museum in a three-year-old building displays hundreds of artifacts from the industry along with everyday items from daily island life of the past century.

After perusing the artifacts, tourists are invited to don hard hats for a guided tour of #2 Mine, where they may experience briefly what it felt like to work underground all day, in semi-darkness and danger, surrounded by walls of iron.

Tour guides explain how the tunnels extended nearly three miles out under Conception Bay when the mines were working. The shafts were supported only by the dense vein of ore, with tunnels cut in a jagged pattern—angles going in one direction on one wall and the opposite

*Tourists are invited to don hard hats for a guided tour of #2 Mine, where they may experience briefly what it felt like to work underground all day, in semi-darkness and danger, surrounded by walls of iron.*

direction on the facing wall to lend strength. Water was constantly pumped out and oxygen was pumped in for the miners.

But the tunnels under the bay are flooded now. Number 2 Mine was shut down in 1949, while miners were earning 10 cents an hour. Guides say people have reported seeing the ghostly images of miners in the shaft, cleaning the face of the mine or digging with their jackhammers.

Carts and rusted horseshoes mark the shaft's stable area where the ponies and horses that pulled the carts full of ore were stabled permanently underground.

"If they were brought to the surface, they were blindfolded, or they would go crazy and blind," explained summer tour guide Ashley Coombs, an island resident and university student. She would not have been allowed in #2 Mine when it was open. "Women had to stay clear of the mines. They were considered bad luck."

The island's six mines produced 80 million tons of iron during 75 years of operation and a total of 105 men were killed. The strength of the walls in the iron mines made them less susceptible to collapse than shafts where other minerals were mined.

"The miners had a little house for eating lunch, with a stove to heat tea," said Coombs. "On Fridays, they brought in Screech." Screech is a strong, dark Jamaican rum with the map of Newfoundland on the label. Legend has it the rum's name came from the reaction non-Newfoundlanders had when they first tried it.

## THE ONCE AND FUTURE ISLAND

The island's murals are huge, beautiful and impressive and they are attracting visitors, although not yet enough to make tourism a full-fledged, community-supporting industry on the island.

Each summer, however, more tourists board one of the two ferries for the 20-minute trip to Bell Island from Portugal Cove, less than a half-hour car trip from Newfoundland's biggest population center, the capital city of St. John's. On the ferry ride, nature-loving tourists could spot whales, seals or even an iceberg in season.

From the ferry, a large rock called The Pulpit rises from the bay near an island cliff and stands out against the sky.

The Bell is a landmark rock on the other side of the island, next to its smaller neighbor, The Clapper. The island may have been named for the Bell, but another theory says the early French settlers called the island "Belle" for its natural beauty.

Whatever the derivation of the name, Bell Island's mayor and lifelong resident, Gary Goisine, feels optimistic about the future. He is happy that 15,000 people toured the mine shaft last year.

*The island's town is Wabana, the name given to the island by its first residents, meaning "The Place Where the Sun First Shines."*

*Unlike most small communities in Newfoundland, Bell Island—six miles long, two miles wide and situated only three miles off the mainland across The Tickle—was not dependent on the 500-year-old cod fishery that collapsed in 1992.*

"I'm in the moving business. Years ago, my uncle moved a lot of people from Bell Island to Cambridge, Ontario," Goisine said. "Forty years later, I'm moving a lot of retired people back home to rural Newfoundland. People are being appreciative of their roots." He believes retirees long for the solitude, peace and hospitality of rural life. "Those who come back to Bell Island know they can go borrow a teabag from their neighbors."

"I just moved a lady from Ontario to Bell Island," added Goisine. "She wasn't a former resident. She found it on the Internet."

Every Christmas, Goisine moves more than people. He drives seven days to make a Christmas delivery to Cambridge, bringing islanders' gifts and homemade baked goods to their distant relatives and supplying the homesick expatriates with their favorite brands of Newfoundland-brewed beer. "Black Horse is the first choice, followed by Blue Star, and some Dominion."

Ken Kavanagh, the retired teacher, believes he was lucky to be the oldest of 14 in his family, because when he graduated from college, he found the Bell Island teaching job he kept until retirement. His siblings had to leave to find work. He believes only its proximity to St. John's saved Bell Island from the total abandonment most Newfoundland islands experienced during resettlement.

He doesn't expect any of his own four children will ever return to live on the island, but his daughter, Heidi—like more than half the teachers on the island now—commutes from St. John's to teach there every day. Four schools have been reduced to three and former teacher Kavanagh, now a school trustee, may have to participate in the painful decision to close another one.

When the mines closed, his father, like many other island men, was ruined. The provincial resettlement offer did him no good. "My father, with 14 kids and no education, couldn't go anywhere," said Kavanagh. "I saw so many broken families, alcoholic fathers, devastated mothers... The shutdown created a dysfunctional economy, dysfunctional families and a dysfunctional community."

To help save the island, Kavanagh became active in community development. He asked the premier to hold a meeting there to witness the devastation. ("I was naive.") He helped form a committee that held kitchen meetings for three years, formed a co-operative and planned projects. The group helped start a bakery, still operating on the island, and a senior citizens' complex. It was slow going and the original members have burned out, but he says he's still hopeful.

"There's still a strong core of Bell Island families," said Kavanagh. "Many are coming back and buying summer homes. But there has to be a reason for young people to stay, and that's got to be a job."

An entrepreneur recently opened a seafood plant on the island, mostly processing sea urchins for the Japanese market. He employs 60 people. A Bell Island native moved home to open a business manufacturing highly specialized scaffolding used in the hydro industry and oil refineries that will employ 10.

"We have more than 400 jobs in town," said the mayor. "More than 300 residents commute to St. John's every day. They brave all the weather; sometimes the boat breaks down. They have to line up as early as 5 a.m. and sometimes don't get home until 7 p.m. They put in a 14-hour day to get paid for seven and a half."

Development director Connors says the two Bell Island ferries carry 450,000 passengers and 225,000 cars annually—more passengers than the huge Marine Atlantic ferry service that brings people from the mainland to Newfoundland.

Americans are buying houses and land on the island. A developer is considering a 75-home subdivision. "I think we will become a thriving town," said Goisine. "The security is great. The people are great. With a couple more businesses we should be okay."

If Connie Kelloway gets her way, she'll be providing a couple of businesses, at least in the summer. She's brimming with ideas and can't find time to do it all. Everywhere she looks on the island, she sees tourist possibilities. Having a baby slowed her ambitions down, a little.

"I have lots of plans for Bell Island," said Kelloway, 33. Not a native islander, she married a Bell Islander and together they operate a school bus service on the island and in St. John's.

In the summer of 2002, she launched the first visitors' bus tour service on the island, which includes a meal and the mine tour. Startup costs meant the first season wasn't profitable, but she expects next year it will pay off. "I had a great time doing it. We had lots of people. I can't wait till next summer to do it again."

*Nancy Griffin, a Maine-based freelance writer, is a native of Newfoundland.*

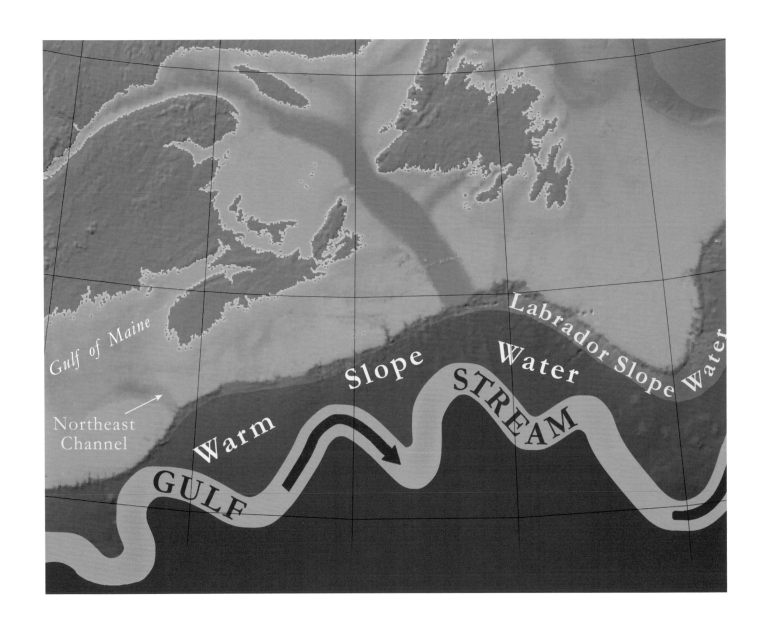

Gulf of Maine

Northeast
Channel

Slope

Water

Labrador Slope Water

Warm

GULF

STREAM

# *Time, Space,*
# *Oceans*
# *and Climate*
# The North Atlantic Oscillation

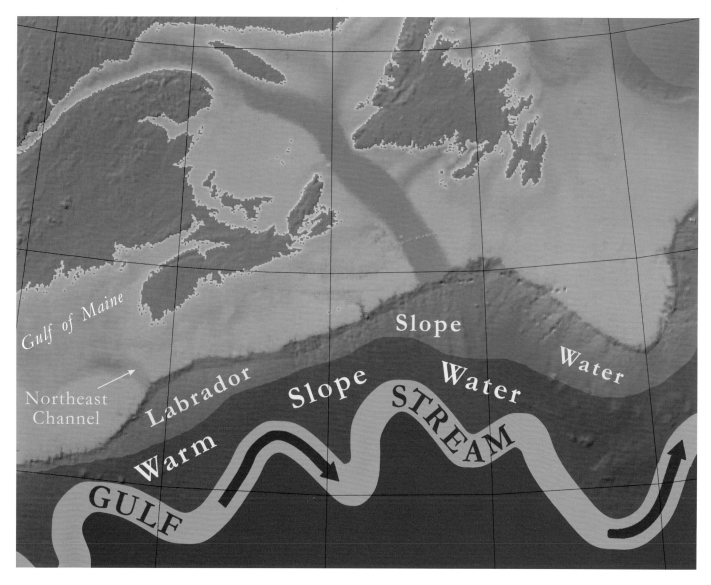

Gulf of Maine

Northeast
Channel

Slope

Water

Labrador Slope Water

Warm Slope Water

GULF STREAM

DAVID D. PLATT
PHILIP W. CONKLING

*Facing Page: A **weak** NAO index is characterized by a more southerly track of the Gulf Stream, which allows cold Labrador Slope Water to move further west and south. This slope water is not present at the surface; it is found at a minimum of 200 to 300 meters in depth. So as it moves westward, the relatively shallow Scotian Shelf and Georges Bank that comprise the Continental Shelf in this region block it from coastal waters. Between these features lies the Northeast Channel. More than 200 meters in depth, the channel provides an opening for these cold slope waters to enter the Gulf of Maine.*

*Above: A **strong** NAO index is characterized by a more northerly track of the Gulf Stream that prevents Labrador Slope Water from influencing the Gulf of Maine.*

*Maps by Chris Brehme, Island Institute. Adapted from Ken Drinkwater, Bedford Institute of Oceanography, 2002.*

Scientists have coined a term to underscore how seemingly small and unrelated events in the natural world can have global consequences: the "butterfly effect." The idea is that the flap of a butterfly's wings off the equatorial coast of Africa, say, can stir a little vertical eddy of wind into the air. And when temperature conditions are just right, this bit of rising air can amplify into a larger and larger area of low pressure that ultimately builds into a hurricane that will wreak havoc on the coast of Florida thousands of miles away.

A common example of the butterfly effect is how the warming of surface waters in the tropical Pacific affects global weather conditions. Known as *El Nino*, this phenomenon affects weather and the presence (or absence) of important schooling fish, seabirds and marine mammals along the west coast of the Americas from Alaska to Chile. Now scientists are focusing on a less well-known Atlantic counterpart to *El Nino*.

The North Atlantic Oscillation—the name applied to this recently understood phenomenon—appears to determine the location and strength of the Gulf Stream and Labrador Current, the warm and cool oceanic "rivers" that, in turn, determine conditions and productivity of places such as the Gulf of Maine.

As in the Pacific, the periodic rise and fall in pressure differences between two atmospheric "cells" over the North Atlantic Ocean appears to be closely linked to the seasonal climate over the entire North Atlantic Basin. The effects are just as large: stronger or weaker storm systems that lead to warmer or cooler ocean temperatures, and ultimately to mild or frigid winters in Europe and North America.

But a lot more than just weather is interconnected here: scientists are beginning to appreciate how the North Atlantic Oscillation can influence disparate events in our daily lives, such as the incidence of red tide in mussels or lobster landings along the Maine coast.

Neal Pettigrew, an oceanographer at the University of Maine and chief scientist for the Gulf of Maine Observing System (GoMOOS), describes the North Atlantic Oscillation as "the largest scale mode of climate variability in the North Atlantic sector," noting that its effects are felt in North America and Europe "from the upper atmosphere to the deep ocean."

Like *El Nino*, the North Atlantic Oscillation (NAO) swings between "negative" (weaker atmospheric pressure differences, fewer and weaker storms, frontal region and storm tracks further south) and "positive" (stronger pressure differences, more and stronger storms, frontal region and storm tracks farther north) on time scales that extend over years.

Indirectly, the NAO also has a major effect on ocean productivity by influencing which ocean current goes where. Variations in the NAO index determine which major current "rivers" enter the Gulf of Maine, a large inland sea connected to the rest of the North Atlantic through a deep entrance called the Northeast Channel. The channel lies between the higher underwater ridges of Brown's and Georges Banks.

When the NAO Index is in a positive mode (meaning that the difference in pressure between the Azores High and the Icelandic Low is greater than average),

storms and weather fronts track further to the north. The Gulf Stream tracks further north as well, bringing warmer winter weather to northeastern North America and northern Europe. It also brings warmer, saltier waters to the Northeast Channel entrance of the Gulf of Maine.

Conversely when the NAO Index is negative, storms and fronts track further south, and colder, fresher waters of the Labrador Current (as well as weather fronts) arrive at the entrance of the Gulf of Maine. The differences between the deep Labrador "slope" waters and the slope waters associated with the Gulf Stream have significant consequences for vast segments of the Gulf of Maine's biological community.

For much of the 1980s and 1990s the NAO Index was positive. But then in 1998, the index dipped sharply negative. It also happened that in 1998, Neal Pettigrew and others studying the oceanography of the Gulf of Maine began to detect cold Labrador Current waters entering the Gulf of Maine through the Northeast Channel, six months after the NAO index began its steep dip. Between June and August of 1998, shipboard observations and moored buoys tracked the spread of these cold bottom waters throughout the deep basins of the Gulf of Maine. Fortuitously, Pettigrew had situated ocean buoys in the shelf waters of the Eastern Maine Coastal Current, offshore from Mount Desert as well as throughout Penobscot Bay. Data from the buoys and observations confirmed that the Gulf of Maine was one to two degrees colder in 1998 than in the preceding and succeeding years. Although they did not know it at the time, Pettigrew and his colleagues had stumbled into a front-row seat to watch a major oceanic event.

In the late spring of 1998, lobstermen who fish in coastal waters between Mount Desert Island and Penobscot Bay caught virtually no lobsters during the period they refer to as the "spring spurt" when lobsters are typically headed to warmer, shallower waters to shed their old shells and mate.

The tantalizing hypothesis: that the colder waters affected the behavior patterns of lobsters.

Pettigrew hypothesizes further that the Labrador slope waters of 1998 could have triggered a cluster of red tide outbreaks along sections of coast west of

Penobscot Bay, a region where outbreaks are comparatively rare. Inshore water temperatures were cooler, likely caused by lower temperatures offshore, along with a change in nutrients. All this was brought about, he surmises, by the NAO.

An abundance of phytoplankton—microscopic plant species like those that cause red tides—can be counted on to attract an abundance of other creatures (resident or migratory fish, marine mammals, bird species) that depend on "primary productivity" to thrive.

The visible effects of shifts in phytoplankton and zooplankton regimes can have an effect on larval lobsters, for example, or schools of herring or groundfish, but these effects may not be apparent immediately.

A "modest 2001 NAO low event," says Pettigrew, "may have important fisheries implications in the next year or two." Similarly, Pettigrew believes, altered water properties in Penobscot Bay and other embayments "may cause differences in lobster larval settlement, timing of lobster shedding and lobster landings."

Pettigrew expects 2003 to be another NAO low, with fisheries implications emerging one to two years in the future. "Conditions far offshore," says Pettigrew, "serve as a forecast of future nearshore conditions."

GoMOOS has already deployed 10 automated buoys around the Gulf of Maine including one in Penobscot Bay. The solar-powered buoys provide real time information via phone or the GoMOOS website (www.gomoos.org) about sea conditions including wind, wave height, temperature, salinity and currents. The present suite of buoys ranges from southeast of Gloucester, Massachusetts, to Saint John, New Brunswick and Yarmouth, Nova Scotia. Pettigrew would add an additional buoy in the Northeast Channel, where the Labrador Current rounds the tip of Nova Scotia northeast of Georges Bank. "A Northeast Channel buoy would provide an early warning system for approaching changes in the interior of the Gulf of Maine," he says.

---

*David D. Platt* is Editor of Island Journal.
*Philip Conkling* is President of the Island Institute.

# *Climate Change, Up Close*

Gary Comer

**P**reviously unknown linkages such as the NAO, often operating over huge geographic scales, can affect ocean currents, weather patterns and fish abundance. Such linkages can also affect wildlife populations. The reproductive failures of terns and boobies during El Nino events in the Pacific Ocean are an example.

Last summer, during an expedition attempting to cross the Northwest Passage from west to east, we saw firsthand how changes in the Arctic Ocean's ice pack changedthe habits of one of the Arctic's most inspiring creatures, *Ursus maritmus*, the polar bear.

At Point Barrow I joined the exploration vessel TURMOIL that had successfully crossed the Northwest Passage the prior year from Baffin Island to Point Barrow, Alaska. The ship had been getting ice reports for months from NOAA's chief ice forecaster. He told us that the warming of the Arctic and the consequent thinning of the Arctic ice pack had resulted in a chunk of ice the size of Indiana breaking off the main ice sheet. He said it was too big to get through the Bering Strait between Alaska and Russia and that it could pose a navigational problem for the expedition.

In fact, the ship and the expedition were pinned in, behind the narrow spit of Point Barrow and the Plover Islands in a small inlet for the first two weeks of August 2002. The ice stretched for hundreds and hundreds of square miles just outside the spit, and we waited for a shift in wind patterns to drive it northward. For the entire time we were pinned down, we were witness to a display of polar bear activity that was remarkable even for northern Alaska. Normally by August, the pack ice along the northern shore of Alaska has mostly melted, allowing maritime transportation to the Alaska oil fields and further west into the central Arctic. As the ice moves offshore, the Arctic cod that feed under the ice margin also move offshore. Seals follow the cod; bears follow the seals.

But this year, with the ice hard aground where the Beaufort Sea meets the North Atlantic coast, nothing was moving. Seal and walrus stayed along the coast, feeding late into the summer. And the bears stayed with them. Every day we were pinned in the inlet, we saw polar bears. After 60 sightings, we became more cavalier about recording them. After 100 sightings, we stopped counting. Why so many bears converged at this one spot, Point Barrow, was not clear, but we identified scores of different individuals.

Thrilling as the sightings were, they were harbingers of a more terrifying story that unfolded after the ice finally gave way. The ice did not just move gradually offshore; when it left, it went in a great hurry and retreated over 100 miles northward. The fabulous concentration of polar bears was suddenly stranded. Some undoubtedly swam across miles of open ocean to find the ice, but others were confused. George Divoky, the ornithologist who has been studying a unique black guillemot colony on Cooper Island for the past 29 years, reported that for the first time ever a polar bear raided the seabird colony and ate every last chick from the summer's cohort. Other bears were stranded on Point Barrow, alarming local authorities, who closed the point to all vehicles. The polar bears threatened town; at least one had to be shot before the ice eventually returned in October.

Fish, seals, seabirds and bears have always had to respond to changes in their environment, as has all wildlife. But the scale and pace of these changes seemed immense and global to those who observed them; the rate of change unlike anything scientists have ever documented.

— Philip W. Conkling

# A SERIOUS EATER OF FISH

## Counting an island's cormorants, at the price of a few chicks

*Story and Illustrations by*
RICHARD J. KING

Ed Kloman, a bespectacled Down East school-teacher, calls the cormorant the "most hated bird in Maine." And among Mainers who regularly see these black birds perched on pilings, he is not alone in his opinion. Since Europeans first arrived, cormorants have been shot for sport, for fish bait, to keep them out of fish net pens and to keep them away from their commercial wild fish. Native Americans and early Mainers collected cormorant chicks and eggs for food. When settlers built homes on offshore islands and established farms and quarries, they pushed out cormorant colonies. Cormorant guano probably smells worse than that of any other seabird, and when cormorants nest in trees, their feces kill the foliage and then the trees themselves. Some ecologists attribute the grassy, bald character of several Maine islands to former cormorant colonies.

In the spring of 2001 I traveled to Stratton Island as part of a large study of cormorants. Stratton sits in Saco Bay, less than two miles off Prout's Neck. I served as an Audubon Society research assistant, a guest in residence to learn about ornithological research methods and to peek at the cormorant in its Maine habitat. Under the tutelage of island supervisor Hilary Cerny and warden Sean Donaghy, I spent six days on Stratton.

BRAVE RESEARCH TEAM
9·20·01
MYSTIC, CT USA.

91

Stratton Island is a 35-acre pile of rocks that supports patches of forest and wetland and a few strips of sandy beach. One of these strips is open to the public and has a boardwalk for observing the birds. The National Audubon Society assigns wardens to live on Stratton from late spring through the fall. These wardens, with the help of a few research assistants, monitor the sanctuary's terns, gulls, herons, ibises, eiders, oystercatchers, cormorants and other migrant species. They count the cormorants on Stratton and nearby Bluff Island once a year from an inflatable boat.

The Audubon Society staff stay in tents and cook on a propane stove or in a tiny brick oven. They wash their dishes in the surf, use a composting privy, and read at night by lantern. I helped with the census of waterbird chicks and the construction of a new lean-to, but for most of my visit I observed, sketched, and photographed the cormorants from a low tide rocky shore and from a dome-shaped, camouflage pattern blind.

We set up the blind just back from the edge of the cliff where the cormorants nest. Sitting on an overturned bucket, I peered out the blind's windows. These windows had Velcro and string closures and are more intended for rifles than binoculars. The birds forgot about me once I was inside the blind.

Ed Kloman and other Mainers also call cormorants shags, crow ducks, sea turkeys, sea lawyers and a few unprintables. Ornithologists differentiate two species of cormorants that nest on the Maine Islands. The more abundant Double-crested Cormorant (*Phalacrocorax auritus*) appears all black and has an orange beak and a green eye. The Great Cormorant (*Phalacrocorax carbo*) is larger, a richer black and, when breeding, has a white patch on its thigh. Juveniles of both species have whitish-brown breasts.

The cormorants that nest on Stratton are Double-crested. At the start of June, I saw many of the birds still in their breeding plumage, so their feathers were glossy black with iridescent greens and purples. On a few of their heads, two tufts of feathers fluffed out on both sides. These feathers grow on both males and females and are the reason for their common name,

"double-crested," and probably for their scientific species name *auritus*, which means "eared" in Latin. When an individual with these feather tufts faced directly at me and my binoculars, he or she looked like a frazzled old professor.

Cormorants have long necks, four webbed toes and sharp hooks at the end of their beaks, all for nabbing prey underwater. Cormorants eat mostly fish, but they are opportunistic feeders, meaning they will eat whatever is present, including crabs, small rays, small lobsters, small frogs, insects, shrimp and eels. Most scientific studies show that cormorants do not focus on, or even prefer, commercial fish species, unless these fish, like salmon, are laid out in front of them in abundance, as often occurs at aquaculture facilities or at fish stocking and fish hatchery release sites.

The cormorant's ability to catch fish has got the bird into trouble, both historically and in recent years. In order to protect fish stocks, the U.S. Fish and Wildlife Service destroyed almost 180,000 eggs on the islands of Maine from 1944 to 1953. Since 1972 cormorants have been federally protected, but in 1998, recreational fishermen on Lake Ontario shot approximately 2,000 cormorants to defend their fish stocks. Recreational fishermen on Lake Huron raided a rookery a few years later. One Huron fisherman told *The New York Times* in 2001, "I'd pull the troops out of Afghanistan and napalm the [cormorant] rookeries." Several areas around the country have received permits to either harass or kill cormorants to protect their aquaculture sites, to protect their recreational fishing grounds or to move cormorants out of the habitats of threatened bird species.

Before the end of 2003, the Fish and Wildlife Service will complete a new plan to manage growing Double-crested Cormorant populations around the country.

According to Fish and Wildlife and independent ornithologists, Maine cormorants hit their peak in the 1980s. In contrast to some other parts of the country, Double-crested Cormorant populations are currently declining in Maine, although the state still holds the largest nesting population on the U.S. East Coast. The best and most recent estimates are that 17,000 breeding pairs of Double-crested Cormorants live in 117 colonies along the coast.

Stratton has a modest population of approximately 120 breeding pairs of Double-crested Cormorants, which fluctuates from year to year. On Stratton, the cormorants nest on the rocks of a cliff on the northeast corner of the island. Warden Sean Donaghy and I counted their nests, as well as their eggs and their

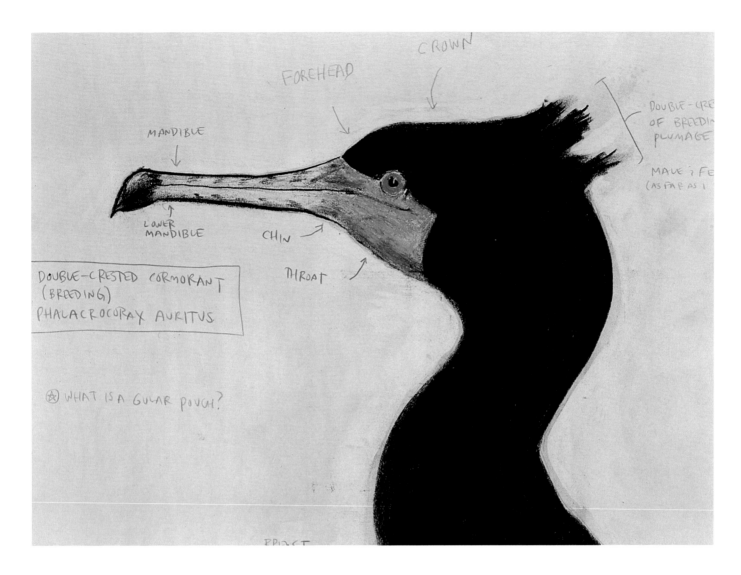

MANDIBLE

LOWER MANDIBLE

FOREHEAD

CROWN

CHIN

THROAT

DOUBLE-CRESTED CORMORANT (BREEDING)
PHALACROCORAX AURITUS

⊛ WHAT IS A GULAR POUCH?

DOUBLE-CRE
OF BREEDIN
PLUMAGE

MALE & FE
(AS FAR AS )

new chicks, featherless and lizard-like. The nests held between one and six eggs and as many as four grasping chicks. Cormorants make their nests with sticks, eelgrass, seaweed, crab shells, fishing line or whatever is available.

Our count took less than 40 minutes, but our disturbance of the colony caused the death of at least three chicks. The Herring Gulls and Black-Backed Gulls swoop in and eat cormorant chicks if there is any disturbance, human or otherwise. Cormorants are timid, quick to fly away and slow to return to their nests. I have since seen gulls eat a cormorant fledgling that was almost as large as they, and, while I was on Stratton, we watched a gull kill and eat a Glossy Ibis that was several inches taller. The Audubon Society and I wanted to get an accurate count of the number of cormorants on Stratton, and so we paid a cost in dead chicks. Humans, gulls and bald eagles are the cormorant's only major predators in Maine.

In the channel between Stratton and Bluff Island, I watched the cormorants fish. Double-crested Cormorants do not hunt from the air, but land in the water and dive from the surface. Cormorants are deep divers. Off the Isles of Shoals, a SCUBA diver told me that he found a dead cormorant in a lobster trap set in over 100 feet of water. Cormorants usually forage within a few miles of the coast, but both Maine species migrate a great distance. A Double-crested Cormorant might winter in any state along the southeast coast, along the Gulf of Mexico or as far south as Belize.

In the channel a cormorant brought a fish back up to the surface, as if taunting the fisherman hand-lining nearby. The cormorant adjusted the fish in its mouth so it went down head first and the spines did not catch along its neck.

It is difficult to determine exactly which species and how many fish cormorants eat. The ornithologists on Stratton and elsewhere explain that cormorants might affect certain fish stocks, but the birds would not stay in an area where there aren't fish. The cormorant's diet is diverse, and perhaps the ecology of a system relies on these birds to eat diseased fish, cull slower fish or eat fish that would prey on our desired commercial fish. The cormorant's presence—and its feces—returns nutrients to the water.

On the fourth day of my visit, it rained throughout the day with cold easterly gusts. I went out to the blind. The gulls stood behind the cormorants on the cliff, as if waiting, or perhaps this is just their normal station. The cormorants both sat and stood, black and quiet, twisting their necks back and laying their head between their wings. Though it was raining and bitter, as if to stretch, one Double-crested Cormorant pulled his neck straight up and spread his wings and held them open. After a few moments the cormorant flew off from the lower rocks of the cliff, falling towards the water, dipping its tail, beating its wings hard to create enough lift. Ed Kloman told me that many of his grandfather's generation thought that a cormorant needed to wet its tail to be able to fly. "It's tough to deny what you see with your own eyes," Ed Kloman said looking over his glasses, "but ideas change. Slowly, but they change."

*Richard J. King is a Teaching Fellow for the Maritime Studies Program of Williams College and Mystic Seaport.*

# FROM THE HELM

*Continued from page 5*

interest of the legislature, which is after all a group of representatives from Maine's constellation of small towns.

At the other end of the archipelago, the Town of Cranberry Isles, comprised of Great Cranberry, Islesford and Sutton Islands, has just produced a compelling new strategy for securing its future. After years of being squeezed out of mainland access points and docks on Mount Desert's shores, the town has purchased a foothold on the Manset side of Southwest Harbor that will provide Cranberry Isles with a vital mainland link. Across the bay, Swan's Islanders dug deep at town meeting this winter to come up with the funds for continuing a community music program begun by an Island Institute Fellow, Candyce Dunham, and embraced by her 117 students aged 2 to 85. At Frenchboro the last house in its seven-unit affordable housing program went under contract this spring. Even more important, the school has new young students and along with the church, year-round running water. Speaking of schools, Matinicus reopened its school after a two-year hiatus to enroll a single student—a nearly incredible testament to the community's resolve to keep taxing itself to maintain the school program even in the absence of students.

In the middle of the archipelago, Monhegan Islanders have come together and successfully raised substantial new funds for the Monhegan Sustainable Community Association, to acquire real estate for affordable housing for year-round residents. Vinalhaven has opened the doors on its stunning new K-12 school with its spacious performing arts center and library. The new school began with the vision of committed group of young islanders who want to raise their kids there, was advanced by a heroic effort on the part of its superintendent and aided by an amazing private fundraising effort. The entrance of the new school is graced by a sculptural granite wall built from locally donated granite, erected by a volunteer crew of island builders and artisans.

Across the Fox Islands Thorofare on North Haven, the news is even more encouraging. The Waterman's Community Center is now fully underway and will anchor what had become a lonely downtown made darker this winter by the closing of the only store along the harbor. The North Haven Historical Society won a prestigious national grant that will help it expand its facilities, and the school continues to produce excellent scholars and young islanders who contribute to the vitality of the community as actors, young scientists and gig racers (rowing vessels that dot the bay in annual races).

Islesboro, Peaks and Vinalhaven are all partners in an innovative project funded by the National Science Foundation to pilot the use of Geographic Information System (GIS) technology—meaning computer mapping techniques—to visualize strategies for managing growth and protecting their islands' natural resources. Great Diamond Island, Maine's newest (and 15th) year-round island community, is experiencing growth pains as islanders struggle to contend with vehicle restrictions—but is making progress. Meanwhile new Island Fellows are working or headed to communities such as Cliff Island in Casco Bay and the working waterfront communities of Stonington-Deer Isle and Friendship along the peripheries of Penobscot Bay.

New coalitions and collaborations, large and small, are flourishing. Islanders have asked for help in forming an Islanders Coalition that they hope will increase their effectiveness at the legislature and among state agencies. A Working Waterfront Coalition is forming to address the complex issues of how to keep diverse uses of the waterfront alive against the rising tide of expensive seasonal residential development that drives out many traditional uses. A group of private island owners has developed a new website to share information about the challenges and charms of living "off the grid" and (almost) completely on your own.

Maine's island realm certainly faces daunting challenges, but the depth of the commitment, energy and passion for keeping Maine's unique island and coastal communities from looking like everywhere else on the Atlantic coast is, in my opinion, more than up to the challenge.

# ALEWIVES

*Continued from page 75*

Bunker took a lot of the credit for its defeat, with an effort that some of his fellow legislators called "strong-arming."

"We ultimately killed the reintroduction of alewives into the St. Croix River, which was what the local people in Washington, Hancock and Penobscot county was hoping we would do," said Bunker, the day the legislation went down.

———

By the spring of 2002, the alewife run on the St. Croix river had plummeted to one thousand fish. At its height in the 1980s, it was up to more than two and a half million. The Canadians for a second year in a row trucked a relatively small number of fish around the barrier, but it's unclear whether their effort will be enough to save the dwindling population of St. Croix river alewives. Through the summer, the Federal government maintained its position that it would withhold needed funding for the state if the barriers weren't removed. But by last December, the feds had backed down. The alewives were on their own.

Many questions remained. On an international boundary river, for example, did the Maine Legislature have the right to act unilaterally in a manner that would affect a resource ostensibly shared with Canada? The Canadians said "no" to that, but have evidently chosen not to pursue the issue further for now. Were alewives really responsible for the crash of smallmouth bass up in Spednic lake? State fisheries officials said "no" to that, but guides in Washington County say the jury's still out on the question. Who makes natural resource policy in the state of Maine? Clearly, in this case, it was the legislature—under severe pressure from the Downeast lobby—not the scientists and resource specialists paid by the state to help formulate that policy.

Has an introduced species been favored over a native one? The Coastal Conservation Association's Pat Keliher thinks so.

"The legislature has chosen to ignore a native species in a major tributary that is an extremely important piece of the pie as far as the Gulf of Maine is concerned. They've nearly eradicated a native species from a Maine river. Their arguments are really skewed toward their own economic benefit, not the benefit of a native species."

And in the polarization that is a hallmark of Maine's natural resource conflicts, Washington County fishing guide Louie Cataldo sees the issue in precisely the opposite terms. If the native alewives pose a threat to the introduced bass that support this region's economy, then the alewives need to go:

"They upset the ecosystem that we've built our business around for the last hundred years; we can't afford to have anything screw it up because we depend on it for our livelihoods."

In the end, oddly enough, both sides agree about what happened: the St. Croix River's native alewives have been condemned to possible extinction because they simply aren't worth as much as an introduced species.

*A former reporter for Maine Public Radio,* **Naomi Schalit** *is now with Maine Rivers.*

# Holy Places

*Sea Room: An Island Life in the Hebrides*
*By Adam Nicolson*
*New York: North Point Press, 2001*
*375 pp., $27.00*

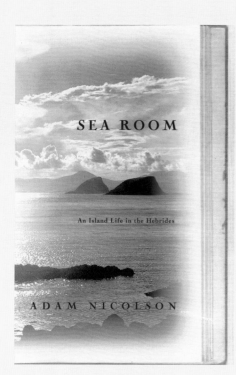

**Reviewed by David D. Platt**

The peculiar geography of islands gives them unusual characteristics. "History collapses," Adam Nicolson asserts, meaning that different eras and times seem to coexist. Amid the raucous sounds of birds and the sea, there is silence. Isolated, the land itself becomes larger in the minds of those who would explore it.

Adam Nicolson inherited the Shiant Islands, off the coast of Lewis in the Hebrides, about 20 years ago. His father had bought them 40 years earlier and gave them to Adam when he turned 21. Now Adam intends to give them to his son Tom when he reaches the same age.

Inhabited today only by sheep and their seasonal shepherds, huge flocks of seabirds and a fair number of rats, the Shiants were once home to "crofters" who eked out a living from its peaty soil. There are ruins on the islands dating from the Bronze Age.

Nicolson sets out in *Sea Room* to explore his relationship to these islands and what it means to "own" them, particularly as an absentee landlord, a writer who makes only brief visits.

"The English landowner," he writes, "is an alien, part joke, part irritant, a tourist who thinks he has some claim on the place." He describes the arrangement between himself and Hughie McSween, who paid him for the right to graze his sheep on the islands. "He became, technically, my tenant. But the reality was different—he was the master and I the pupil. I always felt embraced by his presence."

"I may be in possession of the deeds of the Shiants," he writes. "I may love them more than anywhere else on earth, but I do not feel that I have anything resembling an exclusive right to them, or that any landlord could ... Land—particularly land that is out on the edge of things, and particularly land that is a rich concentration of the marvels of the natural world—is to be shared." His book, Nicolson declares, "is an attempt to share the Shiants."

He delves deeply into their past, exploring the idea that history, in a place such as the Shiants, runs side by side with the present. "The gathering of the Shiants' sweet water ... always feels to me like an engagement with one of the oldest layers of the place," he writes. "It is as if time has not passed ... history does not move here in a single current, sweeping everything up into one comprehensive pattern of change, but in a laminar flow, different sheets of time moving at different rates, one above the other, like the currents of the sea ... gather the water at the well and you are performing a Bronze Age act. Dig over the peaty soil in the vegetable garden and you are doing what has been done here in the Middle Ages. Call Sarah on the mobile phone and you are doing something that wasn't possible until the late 1990s ... [this] is a place in which many different times coexist."

There is wildlife here, in subarctic profusion. Puffins—"ludicrous and lovable ... their sociability is as stiff as an evening in Edwardian London. Gestures of deference are required of any newcomer ... more capable of looking embarrassed than any bird I have ever seen." Gannets—"the fuselage rises on stiletto wings, hangs coolly for a moment, a hundred feet above the sea, and then falls, the body twisting as it goes down, a quarter-revolution or so. There is a sudden half-folding of the wings, a darting of the form, and the bird cuts into the water. The sound is of a paper bag being popped." Shags (cormorants)—"nothing can really prepare you for the shag experience. It is an all-power meeting with an extraordinary, ancient, corrupt, imperial, angry, dirty, green-eyed, yellow-gaped, oil-skinned, iridescent, rancid, rock-hole glory ..."

If "islandness" can be said to be tangible, Nicolson is face to face with it. "Islands feed an appetite for the absolute," he writes at the start of a chapter on the hermits and holy men who gravitated to the Shiants and places like them in the Middle Ages. "They are removed from the human world, from its business and noise. Whatever the reality, a kind of silence seems to hang about them. It is not silence, because the sea beats on the shores and the birds scream and flutter above you. But it is a virtual silence, an absence of communication which reduces the islander to a naked condition in front of the universe. He is not padded by the conversation of others."

Islands, Adam Nicolson knows, are indeed holy places.

# ISLAND INSTITUTE
*Sustaining the Islands and Communities of the Gulf of Maine*

*Since 1983 the Island Institute's mission has been to provide programs and services that help sustain the islands and communities in the Gulf of Maine, comprised of people who depend on each other and on the resources of the sea.*

*Island life is all about collaboration—between those who earn their living with a boat and a buoy, and those who may be guided by a computer or a satellite. The Institute's programs reflect the delicate balance between man and Nature, blending biology and sociology with today's technology.*

## MEMBERSHIP

The Island Institute currently has more than 4,200 members. All of them believe in helping to sustain Maine's islands and remote coastal communities. Join the Institute and help preserve a way of life for generations yet to come. For further information go to our website, www.islandinstitute.org, and click on "participate."

## BOAT DONATIONS

When it's time to stop boating or perhaps get a new boat, many people choose to donate their boat to the Island Institute. Large or small, sail or power, the Institute will find a new home for your boat, even if we can't use it in our programs. If you would be interested in making such a gift, or know of someone who is, please contact us directly or go to our website, www.islandinstitute.org, click on "participate" and select "boat donations."

## PLANNED GIVING

Contributing to the Island Institute through planned giving can provide a significant tax break for the donor while at the same time sustaining the communities and environment of the Gulf of Maine. A gift may generate a better return as a charitable donation than as a highly appreciated asset in your portfolio. The Island Institute offers a variety of planned giving options suited to your needs.

## FELLOWS

This program is designed to provide support to island communities through the efforts of recent college graduates who want to serve in Maine's island and coastal communities while gaining valuable field experience. These one- to two-year placements offer graduate-level students an opportunity to gain community development skills while living on one of Maine's year-round islands. To date the program has placed 27 Fellows in 11 communities, where Fellows work with a variety of community organizations on projects related to environmental and marine science, education and other areas, all determined by the community. Fellows are also expected to ensure that the skills and projects they bring to their host community will continue after their departure.

*Fellows and Institute staff, Chebeague Island, September, 2002.*

Examples of community projects:

- Assisting with islands' comprehensive planning

- Conducting marine research in collaboration with fishermen and cooperating organizations

- Designing and implementing new curricula in island schools

- Writing grant proposals to support new technology and equipment in schools and libraries

- Automating and expanding programming for island library collections

- Providing technical training to island students and adult learners

*For further information about these and other projects, go to the Institute's website, www.islandinstitute.org, and click on "learn more."*

## ISLAND INSTITUTE
386 Main Street, Rockland, Maine USA 04841 • Toll Free (800) 339-9209 • Phone (207) 594-9209
email institute@islandinstitute.org **www.islandinstitute.org**

# ISLAND INSTITUTE MEMBERSHIP BENEFITS

❖ **ISLAND JOURNAL**
Our annual publication, featuring island life, the arts, stories, photographs, essays, poetry, people and marine science.

❖ **WORKING WATERFRONT / INTER-ISLAND NEWS**
A monthly newspaper for and about islands and their communities and resources, with an emphasis on marine industries and the coastal economy. Also accessible on-line at <www.workingwaterfront.com>.

❖ **10% discount at the Island Institute store, ARCHIPELAGO**

ISLAND INSTITUTE • PO BOX 648, 386 MAIN ST., ROCKLAND, ME 04841 • (207) 594-9209 • <www.islandinstitute.org>

# ISLAND INSTITUTE PUBLICATIONS

## 2003 Island Journal, Volume 20
When Hollywood comes to the coast; Maine island artists; Sal and Jane grow up; counting cormorants on Stratton Island; a Newfoundland community survives economic disaster; leadership on Swan's Island; *Working Waterfront* turns 10 ...  $16.95

### The Time of My Life By Emily Muir
A Maine artist and designer tells the story of her long and fascinating life. Muir's own memoirs are interspersed with color and black & white reproductions of her artwork. 130 pages. **SC** $19.95

### Island Institute Posters
*Shown:* **Peter Ralston's "Pentecost"**
*Also available:* **"Sun Dog"**
*(See reverse side for details)*

### Lobsters Great & Small
**By Philip Conkling/Anne Hayden** • How a unique collaboration of more than 100 lobster fishermen, scientists and public agencies investigated *Homarus Americanus*, the American lobster, in Penobscot Bay. Profusely illustrated with color photographs, maps and other graphics. 132 pages. **SC** $24.95

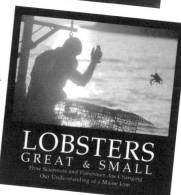

### Working Waterfront/ Inter-Island News
One year (11 monthly issues)
$10.00

### The Coast of Maine from Space
The Island Institute's newest poster is a striking, full color, highly detailed, 24" x 36" image of the coast of Maine (excerpted above) from a satellite image processed by the Institute's GIS department.  $20.00